To Meet Oscar Wilde

A play

Norman Holland

Samuel French — London
New York - Toronto - Hollywood

Copyright © 1999 by Norman Holland
All Rights Reserved

TO MEET OSCAR WILDE is fully protected under the copyright laws of the British Commonwealth, including Canada, the United States of America, and all other countries of the Copyright Union. All rights, including professional and amateur stage productions, recitation, lecturing, public reading, motion picture, radio broadcasting, television and the rights of translation into foreign languages are strictly reserved.

ISBN 978-0-573-01948-7

www.samuelfrench.co.uk
www.samuelfrench.com

FOR AMATEUR PRODUCTION ENQUIRIES

UNITED KINGDOM AND WORLD
EXCLUDING NORTH AMERICA
plays@samuelfrench.co.uk
020 7255 4302/01

Each title is subject to availability from Samuel French, depending upon country of performance.

CAUTION: Professional and amateur producers are hereby warned that *TO MEET OSCAR WILDE* is subject to a licensing fee. Publication of this play does not imply availability for performance. Both amateurs and professionals considering a production are strongly advised to apply to the appropriate agent before starting rehearsals, advertising, or booking a theatre. A licensing fee must be paid whether the title is presented for charity or gain and whether or not admission is charged.

No one shall make any changes in this title for the purpose of production. No part of this book may be reproduced, stored in a retrieval system, or transmitted in any form, by any means, now known or yet to be invented, including mechanical, electronic, photocopying, recording, videotaping, or otherwise, without the prior written permission of the publisher. No one shall upload this title, or part of this title, to any social media websites.

The right of Norman Holland to be identified as author of this work has been asserted in accordance with Section 77 of the Copyright, Designs and Patents Act 1988.

CHARACTERS

Oscar Wilde, an exile
Lord Evelyn, another exile
Penelope Dyall, an actress
Newsboy

The action of the play takes place in a lecture hall near the Rue des Beaux Arts, Paris

Time: 11th October 1899

To Meet Oscar Wilde received two premieres, in Germany and in England. David Carr, a former Hollywood actor, gave a splendid performance in an award-winning production (the German/English Theatre Award) at the German English Theatre which had been converted from a church where Queen Victoria worshipped when she visited Germany.

Vicki Lane's production for the Club Theatre in Altrincham increased the cast to six, which provided a greater intensity and focus on Wilde. Her arrangement was as follows:

Oscar Wilde	Guy Torrance
Lord Evelyn	Kevin McCabe
Lord Alfred (Bosie)	
Frank Harris	
Lord Queensberry	
Sir Edward	
A Member of the Public	
Oliver Elton	
Davey Cross (a convict)	
Fingers Bennett (a convict)	
Chaplain	
Major Nelson	
Martin (a warder)	
Major Isaacson	David Eastwood
Barrister	
Miss Penelope Dyall	Melanie Davy
Lady Mandrake	
Lady Wilde	
Constance Wilde	
Miss Blanche Garland	Francesca Rabar
Newsboy	Daniel Butcher

Casting is flexible.

AUTHOR'S NOTE

It is my intention that this play should be listed as a three-hander and that the Newsboy should be an optional addition. If there is nobody available to play the Newsboy, then the news, like so much else in the play, can be shouted off stage.

The director will evolve his own means of establishing the various characters played by Penelope and Evelyn. The following suggestions are offered merely as a base for registering characterisation. As Constance Wilde, Penelope could wear a large off-the-face hat and, as Blanche Garland, a brightly-coloured toque. Evelyn could make the following adjustments and additions: a rakishly worn silk hat as Bosie; a low-crowned bowler and a walking stick as Queensberry; a black gown for the barrister; a red robe for the judge; a flat cap and scarf for the Man on Clapham Junction railway station; a convict's cap for the two prisoners; a moustache as Major Isaacson to differentiate him from a clean-shaven Major Nelson; a peaked uniform cap as the waiter.

NH

**For Vicki Lane
and
Roger Holland**

ACT I

The setting suggests a lecture platform

A small table is LC, *with two chairs behind it. On the table is a water bottle and glass, a slim volume, a paper knife, pen and inkstand. Another small table is* R, *with a single chair behind it. On this table is a lorgnette, a fan, a notebook and pencil, writing paper, a pen and inkstand. There are entrances* L *and* R

Lord Evelyn, immaculate in the formal attire of the eighteen nineties, enters L. *He is in his mid-thirties. He comes forward to survey the audience*

Evelyn Good evening, ladies and gentlemen. Some of you know me as Lord Evelyn which is indeed my name—or part of it. By agreement with my family, I do not, except in necessity, use the rest. After all, they pay me a generous allowance to stay well away from them. So many of you in the audience are, I know, in a similar situation. We are exiled for (*he shrugs*) whatever reason. The most distinguished of our fellowship is surely Mr Oscar Wilde. Many of you know his history but there are those of us who thought it might be of interest to all of us if he were to tell his story in the form of a lecture. We have described this entertainment as a revelation because it combines commentary with confession. Our hope is that it may help each and all of us to bear misfortune with something of Mr Wilde's philosophy. My function will be that of Chairman...

He breaks off as Penelope Dyall, a smartly-dressed woman of thirty or thereabouts enters confidently L, *walks across the platform to the table* R *where she sits*

Evelyn regards her irritably as he completes his introduction

...will be that of Chairman and I shall be rendering him assistance from time to time. Excuse me. (*He crosses over to Penelope*) Would you mind telling me what you are doing here?
Penelope Since you ask me so politely, I don't mind in the least. I am here by arrangement with Mr Wilde.
Evelyn You are obviously mistaken. Mr Wilde, with my assistance, is about to present a lecture. So, if you will kindly leave the platform...

Penelope I shall do no such thing!
Evelyn (*moving towards her purposefully*) Then I am afraid you leave me no alternative...
Penelope (*rising and raising a hand authoritatively*) Stop!

Evelyn stops. Penelope points into the audience

Do you see the large young man sitting in the fifth or sixth row?
Evelyn (*peering*) I believe I do.
Penelope He is my escort. If you lay a finger on me, I shall not be answerable for your life.
Evelyn (*balking*) Are you threatening me with violence?
Penelope Only as a defensive measure.

Oscar Wilde, impeccable and with a flower in his buttonhole, enters R

Ah, here is Mr Wilde.

Oscar advances to the front of the platform and waves a deprecating hand

Oscar No applause, please. Wait until I have deserved it. (*He turns to the others*) Now just what is going on here?
Penelope ⎫
 ⎬ (*together*) ⎧ The moment I arrived this man asked me to leave——
Evelyn ⎭ ⎩ She just came on and settled herself down——
Oscar (*raising a hand*) One at a time, please. What is it, Penelope?
Penelope I just walked on, sat down and this ... this gentleman threatened to throw me out.
Evelyn She has no business here and I did not wish to hold up the proceedings.
Oscar No business here? On the contrary, she has an important part to play.
Evelyn Then why was I not told? My understanding was that we two were to enact what you described as the main elements of your ascent, decline and fall.
Oscar Quite true. But that was before...
Evelyn If this ... person is to be involved, then I am much afraid that I must withdraw. (*He goes over to the central table and places a chair with its back to the others. Over his shoulder*) Make your choice, Oscar—that woman or myself. (*Pointedly, he folds his arms*)
Oscar (*with a conspiratorial smile at Penelope*) Let me explain—Miss Penelope Dyall is an acclaimed actress of the London stage.
Evelyn (*turning to regard her*) She is?
Oscar Most assuredly. She is here as the emissary from a London manager to discuss a possible revival of my comic masterpiece, *The Importance of*

Act I

Being Earnest, and we thought she could contribute to our undertaking this evening.

Evelyn Oh, if that's the case... (*He rises. Then, with a return of his earlier manner*) But why wasn't I told?

Oscar There just hasn't been the opportunity, my dear fellow. I haven't seen you since Miss Dyall arrived.

Evelyn But we haven't rehearsed. How are we to manage?

Oscar We shall improvise, Evelyn. Now, if I could just effect the introductions... Lord Evelyn, may I present Miss Penelope Dyall?

Evelyn (*icily*) Enchanted to make your acquaintance, Miss Dyall.

Penelope (*equally frostily*) Charmed, I'm sure, Lord Evelyn.

Oscar Now if we could make a beginning. You at the table, Evelyn.

This is the central table at which Evelyn takes his place

And you, Penelope, over there.

Penelope goes over to the other table and seats herself. Oscar turns to the audience

Ladies and gentlemen, I heard Lord Evelyn's introduction and you will have received some impression of our purpose here tonight. It is as both a Bad Example and an Awful Warning that I appear before you and if, in spite of all, you come to some understanding of me, then our time together will not have been wasted. I will begin with a brief description of my antecedents: I am the second son of Sir William and Lady Wilde. My father was the leading otologist and oculist in Ireland and he was a celebrated Irish scholar. My mother was a poet and a revolutionary. You would, of course, expect an extraordinary product of such a union (*with a flourish of his hands*) and here I am. My only sister, Isola, died in infancy and my elder brother fulfilled his early promise...

Evelyn (*rising*) I thought you said that your brother...

Oscar (*waving him back to his seat*) He achieved a drunken mediocrity which was all he ever promised. As for myself, I enjoyed a most successful academic career: I was twice placed in the First Class in the University examinations at Trinity College, Dublin, where I won the Berkeley Gold Medal for Greek and a Classical Scholarship to Magdalen College, Oxford, where I won a Double First and the Newdigate Prize for Poetry.

Evelyn And all with the most becoming modesty.

Oscar I merely tell this as background to what follows. Literary London was unimpressed by my academic successes. However, I wrote poetry and drew attention to myself by an outpouring of observations, comments and epigrams designed to irritate. One specimen will suffice: "I was working on the proof of one of my poems this morning and took out a comma. In the afternoon, I put it back." All this was wonderfully effective. One day I heard a passer-by observe to a friend:

Evelyn (*rising and pointing*) There goes that bloody fool, Oscar Wilde!

Oscar Remarkable how quickly one comes to be well-known! When my poems were published, I sent an inscribed copy to the Oxford Union. When the librarian announced the gift, an undergraduate named Oliver Elton rose to object.

Evelyn (*rising and taking up the slim volume*) It is not that these poems are thin and they are thin; it is not that they are immoral and they are immoral; it is not that they are this and that and they are this and that; it is that they are, for the most part, not by their putative father at all but by a number of deservedly reputed authors. They are by Shakespeare, by Philip Sidney, by John Donne, by Lord Byron and by sixty more. The volume we are offered is theirs, not Mr Wilde's and I move that it be not accepted. (*He throws the volume on the table*)

Oscar What is one to do in the face of rejection in those terms? I did the only thing possible—I ignored it. Without intention, I became the leader of the Aesthetic Movement and, in consequence, became the butt of cartoonists and the like. The notoriety thus aroused led to the offer of an American lecture tour. This proved profitable, interesting and instructive. I learned to defend myself against crude journalists. I learned a measure of diplomacy.

Evelyn Perhaps you would be kind enough to furnish us with examples.

Oscar Examples? H'm... (*He considers*) Well, in the North I proclaimed that the best American poet was Walt Whitman.

Evelyn And the diplomacy?

Oscar Allow me to finish. In the South, I asserted that the South had produced the finest poet in America, Edgar Allan Poe.

Evelyn That sounds very like hypocrisy to me.

Oscar Hypocrisy ... diplomacy ... two inadequate labels to describe a civilised attempt to promote good fellowship and a sense of well-being. I returned to England, visited Paris and resumed lecturing when my money began to run out. It was then that I fell in love.

Evelyn (*derisively*) Fell in love? My own view, based on a close study, is that you were never in love with anybody but yourself. Describe your symptoms so that we may judge for ourselves.

During the following, Penelope takes up her pen and writes busily

Oscar Better than that, I'll quote you the letter I wrote to my adored Lily Langtry: "I am in love with a beautiful girl ... a grave, slight, violet-eyed little Artemis, with great coils of heavy brown hair which makes her flower-like head droop like a blossom and wonderful ivory hands which

Act I   5

draw music from the piano so sweet that the birds stop singing to listen to her."

Penelope pauses to read what she has written

Penelope (*reading*) "My darling Oscar, your letter, your divine, your lovely letter arrived by this morning's post. Merely to see your handwriting on the envelope makes my heart beat faster until I am faint between joy and expectation." (*She punctuates with a deep sigh*) "Then to read what you have written was to find expectation exceeded and joy surpassed. Blessed are the citizens of Edinburgh for they can see and hear you." (*She sighs again and then writes briefly*) "Come to see me as soon as you can or sooner if possible." (*Again, she writes briefly and concludes*) "Surely no two people were ever so much in love as we are. Ever yours, Constance." (*She puts down her pen and stares dreamily before her*)
Oscar I beg your indulgence. All of you here have, at some time, experienced love, passion, desire, infatuation and have been betrayed into extravagance of language. We recovered, descended into the prose of everyday, married and had two delightful boys, Cyril and Vyvyan.
Evelyn But there was disappointment and distress. The lady's jointure was insufficient to support you, your wife and family.
Oscar (*stung*) I never believed that it would and I always intended to provide for my family. It was for that reason I accepted a literary appointment.
Evelyn (*jeering*) You became the editor of *The Lady's World* if that may be described as a literary appointment.
Oscar However much you may deride the post, it kept us until I began to write my plays. Moreover, I left my mark on that magazine.
Evelyn How? How did you leave your mark?
Oscar I changed its title to *The Woman's World*—I always did have a weakness for alliteration. I mentioned my plays. They are my certain passport to immortality and they were the reason for my celebrity ... not so very long ago. I was the darling of the hostesses who looked to me to provide free entertainment for their guests. Bless them, they used to write "To meet Oscar Wilde" on the corner of their invitations. This was an inducement to the more reluctant of their guests. The dear hostesses? In particular, there was Lady Mandrake...

Penelope, in the guise of Lady Mandrake, rises as waltz music begins to play and provides a background for the rest of the following scene. Penelope picks up her lorgnette and now uses it to regard Oscar

Penelope Mr Wilde, it is more than kind of you to grace my little party. One appreciated the many calls upon your time.

Oscar Lady Mandrake, the pleasure, I do assure you, entirely mine. (*He kisses the proffered hand*)

Penelope But you are very naughty, Mr Wilde. So late, so very late, you arrive at my party. Just look at that little clock on the wall.

Oscar (*shaking his finger at her*) Lady Mandrake, Lady Mandrake, how can that little clock on the wall know what the great big golden sun is doing?

Penelope Always so clever, Mr Wilde. An answer for everything. I was afraid the weather had delayed you—so dreadfully unseasonable.

Oscar Ah, yes! The weather! But if it weren't for the snow how could we believe in the immortality of the soul?

Penelope What an interesting question! But what exactly do you mean?

Oscar (*after brief consideration*) I haven't the least idea!

Penelope You really are incorrigible, Mr Wilde. I have been looking forward to discussing *The Importance of Being Earnest* with you. I have now seen it seven times.

Oscar Seven times! I would be grateful for your critical opinion of the play and I should warn you that I can take any amount of criticism as long as it is expressed in terms of praise.

Penelope First, if I may, I would like to hear your own assessment.

Oscar My dear lady, you shall have it. The first act is ingenious, the second beautiful...

Penelope And the third, Mr Wilde?

Oscar ...And the third is abominably clever. Would you disagree, Lady Mandrake?

Penelope By no means. What you say is as true as Gospel. I would only add that I believe it to be the greatest comedy in the English language.

Oscar Dear lady, your voice is music of the spheres and your words sheer poetry. Astonishing...

Penelope What is astonishing?

Oscar That one so young and beautiful should have been vouchsafed such an awe-inspiring vision of the Truth.

Penelope (*shaking her head*) Come along, I want you to meet Canon Carpenter.

Oscar Oh, must I? He has not a single redeeming vice.

Penelope Always so witty, Mr Wilde. It must be a great strain. You look so pale and tired.

Oscar I am tired, dear lady. I am pale—with night-watching.

Penelope Whatever for?

Oscar Sitting up rehearsing my impromptus.

Penelope (*laughing*) Mr Wilde! For one moment I had believed you to be serious.

Oscar I was never more serious. It is a most debilitating experience. The mere polishing of an impromptu can take anything up to three hours.

Act I

Evelyn rises in the character of Lord Alfred Douglas—Bosie

Penelope I'll take your word for it.

Evelyn comes forward until he is observed by Oscar

But I insist that you meet the Canon.

Oscar (*suddenly serious*) A little later, perhaps. Would you kindly excuse me for a moment? There is somebody over there I simply must see.

Penelope (*raising her lorgnette*) Oh yes, I see. I see. (*She gives him a disapproving look and then, spotting another of her guests, moves in pursuit*) Colonel Dacre! Colonel Dacre! (*By signs, she directs the invisible Colonel*) If you're looking for your wife, she's in the conservatory. (*She takes up a position to watch the encounter between Oscar and Evelyn*)

Oscar Bosie...

Evelyn What do you want?

Oscar Only a few words, Bosie. You must not make such terrible scenes. They distress me unutterably ... and you look so dreadful when you're angry—hysterically angry.

Evelyn No worse than you do at this moment—great cow eyes in your white, flaccid face. (*He laughs*) You ought to see yourself.

Oscar Please, Bosie, don't do it. Come and see me at my suite at the Savoy and, please, no more scenes.

Evelyn Don't provoke me then. Don't preach to me. Don't sermonise. It isn't in character.

Oscar places a restraining hand on the younger man's arm but Evelyn thrusts it away

Take your hands off me. Who do you think you are? You don't own me, you know.

Oscar (*embarrassed*) Keep your voice down, Bosie. Everybody is looking at us.

Evelyn I know—and I don't give that! (*He snaps his fingers*) I won't stay here another minute! I'm off. (*And he turns to go*)

Oscar You can't go like that. You must say goodbye to your hostess.

Evelyn I don't have to do anything. Make my excuses. (*He strides away and sheds the character as he sits again*)

Oscar stands looking after him. Then he turns to us

Oscar There is something I must tell you about myself and, if some of you leave when I have spoken, I shall understand. Some time earlier, I had learned what I had long suspected—that I was not bisexual, but homosexual. At first, I was cautious, but, as time passed, I became reckless, shameless. You've seen Bosie—Lord Alfred Douglas—and possibly you have dismissed him as capricious, petulant. Not to me. What wisdom is to the philosopher, what God is to his saint, he is to me. (*A new thought strikes him*) It comes to me at this moment that he always seemed to dominate me. Could it be that this is what I sought—someone to dominate me, to possess me? (*He ponders this new idea*)

Penelope, still as Lady Mandrake, comes over to him

Penelope Are you all right, Mr Wilde? You ... you look ill.
Oscar Ill? No, no. It is just that I am suddenly conscious of my burden.
Penelope Burden?
Oscar The staggering, overwhelming weight of my genius. I simply must rest. I am afraid I must go!
Penelope So soon? But you've only just arrived.
Oscar Dear lady, time is of no consequence on these occasions. You make an eternity and a single minute seem equally timeless.
Penelope And what, pray, is the meaning of that?
Oscar I must confess, Lady Mandrake, that I haven't a notion. But I suspect that I am attempting to be both profound and polite and, in consequence, falling heavily between two stools. If you follow me...
Penelope (*bewildered*) I'm not sure that I do...
Oscar Pray do not distress yourself. It is no matter. (*He bows and kisses her hand*) It was most kind of you to ask me here this evening.
Penelope It was most amiable of you to come, Mr Wilde. Your time, I know, is precious. But you've hardly... That is, you haven't...
Oscar You mean, of course, that I've failed to give my customary performance of scintillating brilliance. I will, I promise, make ample amends on some future occasion.
Penelope Then I'll take you at your word. What about this next Thursday? I am giving a supper party here next Thursday. Do come, Mr Wilde.
Oscar I am so sorry, Lady Mandrake, I regret that I am prevented by a subsequent engagement.
Penelope (*playfully striking him with her lorgnette*) Oh, Mr Wilde! So witty! So devastating! I must hurry and tell Lady Motorchard before anybody else does! (*She turns from him, goes to her table and sits once more*)

The waltz music dies away. Evelyn rises

Oscar Who lived a life as fulfilled as mine? I lived in the glow of my successes, lived for the gratification of the intellect, for prohibited pleasures

Act I

and forbidden ecstasies. But there were undertones of menace, notes of warning. Perhaps if I had listened to my friends, notably Frank Harris.

Evelyn, in the role of Frank Harris moves nearer to Oscar. There is a background of street noises—horses' hooves etc.

Evelyn Oscar...
Oscar Oh, hallo Frank.
Evelyn I saw you the other evening, Oscar.
Oscar I saw you, dear boy. I waved but couldn't attract your attention. It seemed to me that you persistently avoided my eye.
Evelyn Yes. Persistently.
Oscar Frank! Are you serious?
Evelyn I was never more so. I wouldn't be seen dead with such creatures. Where did you find them?
Oscar I didn't. They found me.
Evelyn But how can you tolerate them? How can you endure their company? What are they—posturing page boys or mincing grooms?
Oscar I don't know what they do for a living. They are so very fascinating ... so splendidly, terribly wicked. To be with them is like feasting with panthers.
Evelyn I never saw beings less like panthers and more resembling sheepish, debauched clowns. As I sat at the bar, I saw you give one of them a cigarette case. A silver cigarette case, it seemed to me.
Oscar Oh, yes. I believe I did. I often do that as a pledge of friendship. I like to give presents to young men who please me.
Evelyn Young men who please you! (*He glances uneasily about him*) Don't, please, say such things, Oscar. There are those who would be glad to misunderstand.
Oscar But why not when it happens to be true?
Evelyn As your friend, I must warn you. People are talking.
Oscar Quite unavoidable, my dear Frank. People have tongues. They must employ them—however pointlessly.
Evelyn Shall I tell you what you ought to do?
Oscar By all means tell me what you think I ought to do.
Evelyn You should look elsewhere for your pleasures and satisfactions. You should look to fulfil yourself by taking full advantage of your opportunities. Look at me—successful in all I undertake. I am invited to all the great houses in the country.
Oscar (*nodding*) So you are, Frank. So you are—once.
Evelyn (*unheeding*) My work—my writing—is praised by the foremost critics of the day.
Oscar Indeed, Frank, you have a truly astonishing facility for assimilating

the ideas of the more intellectual of your acquaintance and then presenting them with an impressive and entirely spurious gloss of originality.

Evelyn You are trying to provoke me, Oscar. But I am speaking for your own good. (*He preens*) Finally there is my absolute, complete, total success with women...

Oscar Ah there, Frank. I am bound to agree with you. You have had an overwhelming success with women...

Evelyn (*glowing*) Yes, yes, Oscar.

Oscar ...With the sort of women most of us would pay dearly to keep away from us.

Evelyn (*furious*) That is an outrageous, bloody, bastardising lie! Come with me now—this very instant. I am on my way to a house quite near here where there are women who adore me. (*He kisses his fingertips*) Such women! Such glowing, pulsating creatures! Full-bosomed, generous-hipped, passionate... Why, there's one girl there who...

Oscar Yes, yes. You told me about her. Absolutely disgusting! How you can bring yourself...

Evelyn Very well. Very well, Oscar. Be evasive and flippant if you must but listen to me.

Oscar shows signs of inattention

Listen! People are talking of your association with these revolting wretches. You are seen everywhere with them. There are many who hate you because you are successful and you so obviously enjoy your success. They could make mischief out of your connections with these... these boy bitches. Be discreet, Oscar. Better still, give them up.

Oscar Why Frank! I never thought I would live to hear you preach a sermon!

The sound of hoofbeats and wheels near at hand announce the approach of a cab

But I hardly think you are in a position to instruct me—especially as you have already admitted that you are on your way to a brothel.

Evelyn At least I demonstrate that my instincts are normal. Hey, there! Cab! Cab!

The unseen cab halts and Evelyn runs off in pursuit

In a moment, the cab starts up again and the sound of wheels and hoofbeats recede. Oscar gazes reflectively after the cab

Oscar Normal! Normal! What a thing to boast of! Really, Frank! (*But he is*

Act I

clearly considering the warning) Who could possibly hate me as much as all that?

During the following, Penelope rises and takes the centre of the platform with an assured air. She is carrying the fan with which she makes play from time to time

(*Shrugging, dismissing the mood*) My success in no way surprised my mother, now widowed and living in Chelsea. It delighted her when I attended one or other of her salons. She could be said to bask in reflected glory.

Penelope The kindest of my friends are given to saying that something exciting always happens at Lady Wilde's receptions. This promises to be such an occasion. Oscar, my younger son, is as you all know, as renowned for his writing as for his wit. He has just this moment arrived from a party where he has been entertaining royalty with his flights of fancy and his felicities of phrase. He is now going to speak to us. I want you all, particularly those of you who are young, to treasure this experience for, however long you may live, you will be proud to boast hereafter that you once heard Oscar Wilde, that many-sided genius, speaking at one of his mother's receptions. Oscar, darling, say something brilliant and memorable to us.

She holds out her hands as Oscar strides towards her. He takes her hands in his and kisses her. There is increasing applause as they turn, hand in hand, to face the audience. Then Oscar quells the applause with a gesture similar to that employed by his mother. He steps forward a pace. Penelope remains near him smiling proudly and reacting to Oscar's speech

Oscar Who could possibly live up to the expectations aroused by such a fanfare?

There is some laughter

I must confess I cannot. All mothers are fond and doting—perhaps my dear mother more than most. You heard her just now refer to me as a genius. My friends, it is acutely embarrassing to be praised for something one cannot help. How could I be other than a genius when you consider my parentage? My lamented father was the leading oculist and otologist in Ireland and the foremost in the study of the history, archaeology and mythology of his country. From him I derive a great deal but it is from my mother that I inherit most. From her I inherit my love of beauty, my passion for words and such writing talent as I possess. You know, you must know that my dear mother is famous as Speranza, the greatest poet and patriot of her time. She has been the inspiration, the torch, the hope, the rallying cry for generations of Irishmen. I am now going to ask her for my sake, as well as yours, to recite some of her own poetry.

He takes Penelope by the hand and leads her forward a pace or two before retiring. She strikes an exaggerated attitude and recites her verse in declamatory style to the accompaniment of extravagant and largely inappropriate gestures

Penelope Oh, that I stood upon some lofty tower,
Before the gathered people face to face
That, like God's thunder, my words of power
Roll down the cry of freedom to its base.
Oh! That my voice, a storm above all storms,
Could cleave earth, air and ocean, rend the sky
With the fierce earthquake-shout, "To arms! To arms!"
For truth, freedom, fame, vengeance, victory!

There is an outburst of applause which Penelope acknowledges with a curtsy. Smiling, Oscar moves to her side and takes her hand

Oscar Lady Knowles is beckoning. She wishes, I'm sure, to congratulate you. (*Then, lowering his voice*) Mother, why did you not announce the title of your poem?
Penelope (*smiling up at him*) Dearest Oscar, I had forgotten it.

He leads her over to her chair where she sits. Then he returns to the centre of the platform wearing a concerned expression

Oscar I have already indicated to you that my way of life was known to many and condemned by some. There were those who pointedly avoided my company. Threats hung in the air and now the signs of danger became increasingly apparent.

Evelyn, carrying a walking stick, erupts on to the platform, shouting

Evelyn Wilde! Where are you, Wilde?
Oscar (*turning to face him*) Lord Queensberry! How did you get in?
Evelyn Never mind about that. I am here to discuss a serious matter. You have me to face now.
Oscar So it would appear—and I find it singularly unpleasant.
Evelyn I've no doubt you do. With good reason, sir! (*Suddenly barking*) Sit down!

Oscar *(quite unmoved)* Lord Queensberry, I do not allow anyone to speak to me like that in my own home ... or anywhere else. I suppose you have come to apologise for what you wrote about my wife and myself in that letter you wrote to your son. I ought to prosecute you for writing such a letter.
Evelyn I believed it to be true that your wife was divorcing you.
Oscar Then you will, no doubt, be relieved to hear that you were misinformed.
Evelyn Anyway, the letter was privileged as it was written to my son.
Oscar How dare you write such things about your son and me?
Evelyn I was entirely justified. You *were* kicked out of the Savoy Hotel, at a moment's notice, for disgusting behaviour.
Oscar Someone, it would appear, has been telling you an absurd set of lies about your son and me. I have not, I assure you, done anything of the kind. *(He peers beyond Evelyn)* Who is that out there in the hall?
Evelyn His name is Spike Madden. He is a pugilist and I employ him as a bodyguard.
Oscar Do you now? You can't have felt very sure of yourself when you set out.
Evelyn When one is to treat with scoundrels, one takes precautions.
Oscar Does one? Does one, indeed? I bow to your superior authority and your doubtless wide experience of treating with scoundrels. Lord Queensberry, do you seriously accuse your son and me of improper conduct?
Evelyn I don't say you are at it, but you look it and you pose it which is just as bad. I give you fair warning, Wilde—if I catch you and my son together in any public place, I will thrash you.
Oscar I don't know what the Queensberry rules are governing such encounters but the Wilde rules are to shoot on sight. *(He moves slightly and mimes the pulling of a bell-rope)*
Evelyn It is a disgusting scandal!
Oscar If it is so, then you are the author of the scandal and nobody else. *(Once more, he looks beyond Evelyn to where his servant stands outside our line of vision)* Oh Arthur. This is the Marquis of Queensberry, the most infamous brute in London. Under no circumstances is he ever to be admitted to this house again. *(Then, turning to Evelyn)* Now, get out! *(Then, pointing to the invisible bodyguard)* You too! Get out!
Evelyn *(going)* And I'm glad to go! There is nothing to detain me here! *(He turns at exit R)* But you haven't heard the last of me—not by a long chalk!

Evelyn goes off

Oscar turns to his audience

Oscar This vile man, taunted by his acquaintances about my relationship

with Bosie, was obsessed by his aim to separate us and by his fixed determination to destroy me. In this latter objective, it could be said that he was considerably helped by Bosie.
Evelyn (*off*) Oscar! Oscar!
Oscar (*turning*) Yes, what is it?

Evelyn enters

Evelyn Where are you going?
Oscar Through there. (*He points*) Through the side door.
Evelyn Oh, no, you're not. That would be cowardly. And I am certainly not sneaking in by the side door with you.
Oscar But, Bosie, let us use a little discretion. Suppose your father sees us...
Evelyn Let him. I hope he does. I hope he comes over and makes a scene. Then we'll show him. (*He produces a revolver from his pocket*) We'll see who does the shooting.
Oscar (*alarmed*) Put that away, Bosie. Put it away at once!

Reluctantly, Evelyn does so

Evelyn It's about time we showed him that we're not to be intimidated by his threats. I'm not afraid of this loathsome man. We'll make a royal entrance and, when we do, they'll cease chattering and they'll say: "Look, there goes Oscar Wilde with his ... minion."

Evelyn strides triumphantly off L, calling as he does so

(*Off*) This way, Oscar! This way!

As Oscar unhappily turns to follow him, Penelope rises and, notebook and pencil in hand, calls to him

Penelope Mr Wilde! Mr Wilde!
Oscar (*apprehensively*) Yes, yes. What do you want? (*Then, his face clearing*) But I know you. Just a moment... I have it! You're Miss Blanche Garland and you are employed by *The Woman's World*.
Penelope I used to be employed by *The Woman's World*, Mr Wilde. Now I am a reporter with the *Westminster Gazette*.
Oscar So you are a lady reporter. How very interesting! What can I do for you?
Penelope I won't detain you for more than a few minutes, Mr Wilde. Could I have a few words for my paper?
Oscar They must be very few then, my dear Miss Garland. As you see, I am

Act I

just about to enter my club and this is the time of day when we all sleep most seriously together.
Penelope Mr Wilde, about your new play...
Oscar (*encouragingly*) Yes?
Penelope Our readers are most interested.
Oscar Naturally.
Penelope Do you think it will be a success? (*She writes busily during Oscar's response*)
Oscar My dear young lady, I have written the play and therefore it is bound to be a great success. The only doubtful factor is the audience. Will they be equal to the occasion? Will they be a success? We can only hope... and pray. Is that all, Miss Garland?
Penelope Yes, Mr Wilde. And thank you.
Oscar (*with a grave bow*) Thank you.

Penelope closes her notebook and they both leave the platform by separate exits

For the first time since we began, the platform is empty. Immediately, loud, sustained applause breaks out and there are cries of "Author! Author!" and "Bravo!"

Oscar enters looking highly gratified and holds up a hand to enjoin the silence which quickly follows

Ladies and gentlemen, I have enjoyed this evening *immensely*. The actors have given us a charming rendering of a *most* delightful play and your kind appreciation has been *most* intelligent. I congratulate you on the success of your performance which persuades me that you think *almost* as highly of the play as I do myself.

There is some laughter and renewed applause which dies away as Oscar, now looking grave, once more confronts his audience

There I was relishing what is surely the sweetest of all sounds—deserved applause. Just then I showed the public face. I have told you of my way of life. It was now I felt that I could not live as I wished if I continued to stay in the home I shared with Constance and the boys so I took a succession of hotel suites. Here I conveniently entertained my ... friends, and lived with Bosie. It was a situation fraught with peril and precariously sustained by evasions, deceits, prevarications and lies. Does that sound like an admission or remorse? Dismiss the thought! In my own peculiar fashion, I was enjoying myself.

Evelyn enters as Bosie

Oh, hallo, Bosie. I read your note. It wasn't very explicit.

Evelyn Wasn't it? Then I'll come to the point. Can you let me have some money?

Oscar How much do you want this time?

Evelyn Just whatever you have by you. Twenty ... thirty ... forty ... fifty ... It's just that I want to place a few bets.

Oscar Bosie, you'll have to give up gambling. I just can't afford it.

Evelyn Don't be so bloody mean, Oscar. It was a different story last week. You were pleased enough then to celebrate out of my winnings.

Oscar Winnings! Winnings? Really, Bosie! (*He laughs sarcastically*) What winnings? Remember what you said at the time—one short-priced favourite after a week of unplaced outsiders.

Evelyn You just have to keep on. One has to ride out a run of bad luck.

Oscar (*philosophically*) I suppose one has.

Evelyn (*belligerently*) Are you or are you not going to let me have the money? Racing starts in an hour. I can't wait about here all day.

Oscar I don't seem to have anything on me. (*He pats his pockets*) No. See what there is in the pockets of my dress clothes.

Evelyn Nothing. Not a sou.

Oscar You mean you've looked?

Evelyn Of course.

Oscar Tell me this—if there had been money, would you have taken it?

Evelyn Certainly. You have constantly assured me that what you have is mine.

Oscar How literal you can be, Bosie—when it suits your purpose.

Evelyn Didn't you mean it? Do you wish to go back on your word?

Oscar No, no. Not for the moment. But do, please, be reasonable. The painful fact is that I haven't any ready cash. (*He takes up the pen and scribbles a note*) Look, I've written a note to the theatre. If you will take this round, they'll accommodate you. Only, for pity's sake, bring something back for me.

Evelyn (*snatching up the note and studying it dubiously*) You seriously mean that I'm to take this to the theatre and stand there like a lackey until they've collected, counted and delivered the money?

Oscar If you'd rather go without...

Evelyn Oh, don't be so tiresome! (*Irritably, he stuffs the note into his pocket*) I'll go this time but it is downright humiliating. Really, Oscar, you ought not to find yourself in this sort of situation. Let this be a lesson to you. You ought to keep better control of your money.

Oscar (*nodding*) That may well be. You could be right. But we'll have to draw our horns in soon. I hadn't mentioned it, but, the fact is, we can't leave here because I can't pay the bill.

Evelyn I'm not in the least bit interested in the details. They're your responsibility. Where are we lunching?
Oscar I thought the Café Royal.
Evelyn Oh, very well. The Café Royal at one o'clock. And afterwards?
Oscar Afterwards? Speaking for myself, I'd like to undertake a little cruising.
Evelyn Cruising? Where?
Oscar Oh, around the pubs and dives north of Oxford Street. Last time I picked up that divine creature.
Evelyn From what I saw of him, he was divinely stupid—and none too clean.
Oscar He was representative of the type of young man I choose to patronise in order that they may be afforded a glimpse of a better, more spacious, life.
Evelyn Dear me, Oscar, the pious philanthropist!
Oscar You may mock but I give these young men the benefit of my conversation with some unaccustomed vintage wines and usually some small gift as a memento of the occasion. By the time we part, we have shared a memorable experience. Briefly, they have been dazzled.
Evelyn Not dazzled, Oscar, bemused. They see you as a fat fool mouthing gibberish who plies them with wine when their preference is for beer. As for the memento of the occasion, it is gone as soon as the pawnshops open.

During the following, Penelope, as Constance Wilde, enters carrying a briefcase

Oscar Bosie! Bosie! You would leave me with no illusions if I took you seriously.

Evelyn seems embarrassed by Penelope's advent

Evelyn Oh, good morning, Mrs Wilde. I was just going.

Penelope does not respond to Evelyn's greeting but balefully watches his departure until he has left the stage

Penelope comes over to Oscar who kisses her, almost absent-mindedly, on the cheek

Penelope Good morning, Oscar.
Oscar Good morning, my dear.

She opens her briefcase and takes out a wad of correspondence which she passes to Oscar

Penelope Here you are. I brought your letters.

Oscar (*after a cursory examination of the envelopes*) And a remarkably dull lot they are by the look of them.

Penelope I kept back all the bills as you told me.

Oscar (*patting her arm*) That's my good girl.

Penelope What's to become of them, Oscar?

Oscar Become of them?

Penelope The bills?

Oscar Oh, them!

Penelope There are so many of them. Some have been presented two or three times. There are people who keep coming to the door. The tradesmen, in particular, are becoming impatient.

Oscar It is, my dear, an unfortunate failing of the tradesman. The plebeian hasn't a soul above money. You're keeping all the bills together?

Penelope Oh, yes. Just as you said.

Oscar Splendid! You'll find that they will grow to a wad, a pile, a heap... Finally, to a mound. And then...

Penelope And then?

Oscar One morning you will come down to breakfast and look for them, but you will look in vain for, in their place, you will find an insubstantial mass of burnt paper. Not another thing will be as much as scorched by their burning. The little people do this for their true friends who believe in them and once they are consumed, they are forgotten by everybody—even by the tradesmen.

Penelope You know that isn't true, Oscar. We already have a pile of bills—no, a heap—and I've spent every penny of my allowance. It's worse—a great deal worse—than I've told you. All day long there is an endless procession of people coming to the door and all of them asking to be paid. What am I to do with them?

Oscar Tell them to go away.

She turns angrily away from him

It won't be for long, Constance. We shall have money as soon as I've finished the new play.

Penelope And how long will that be? Just how long do you intend to live here with Bosie? (*She looks around appraisingly*) It must cost a great deal to live in this place.

Oscar (*loftily*) The question of cost, fortunately, does not arise.

Penelope Doesn't it? You can't stay here for nothing—and I'm sure Bosie isn't paying.

Oscar If I am to finish this play, I must have peace and quiet. You must see that, Constance. You have this moment admitted that there is a constant stream of importunate creditors beating on the door. Then there's the children...

Penelope The children! At last you've mentioned them! I was beginning to think that you'd forgotten them. They ask about you all the time. Every day they ask me when you're coming home. I don't know what to tell them!
Oscar My dear...
Penelope Please, Oscar, never mind about the play. Come back to us! Come back soon!

Weeping bitterly, Penelope runs out, snatching up her briefcase as she goes

Oscar follows a little way and calls out

Oscar Constance! Constance! Please don't go! Don't go! Come back! (*He waits for a moment to see if she will return. When she does not, he goes to the table and disconsolately picks up his letters and examines them without much interest. Then he throws them on the table*)

Oscar goes off in the direction taken by Constance

After a moment, Evelyn as Bosie comes in

He looks about obviously seeking Oscar and calls softly

Evelyn Oscar...

He tiptoes about, calls out again and is at length convinced that he is alone. Moving over to the table, he sees the letters, looks left and right for further assurance and then examines the whole pile of correspondence. One of the envelopes obviously interests him and, rejecting all the rest, he holds it up to the light. From the table, he takes a paper knife and, after again glancing about him, he slits open the envelope. He takes out the letter and sits to read it. Clearly, he finds the contents amusing for he laughs as he reads and even more heartily as he turns the page. A noise disturbs him and he restores the letter to its envelope and replaces it on the table. As he is about to move away from the table, he has second thoughts, snatches up the letter and stows it away in an inside pocket of his coat

He is standing, hands in pockets and wearing an expression of studied nonchalance when Oscar hurries in looking greatly perturbed

Oscar is relieved when he sees Evelyn

Oscar Thank heaven you're here. Something terrible has happened. It's this card. (*He takes a visiting card from his pocket and passes it to Evelyn*) Your father left this at my club.

Evelyn studies the card and looks up with an ecstatic expression

See—see what he has written. "Posing as a somdomite." He couldn't even spell the filthy word.

Evelyn That shouldn't surprise you—he's practically illiterate.

Oscar The porter had put the card in an envelope. I don't think he understood it. But the vile, disgusting word has been written and delivered to me. The tower of ivory has been assailed by the foul thing. On the sand my life is spilt.

Evelyn Don't be silly, Oscar. You must see this as an opportunity. We must make the most of it. You want us to stay together, don't you?

Oscar You know I do—more than anything in the world. (*He puts an arm around Evelyn's shoulders*) I want us to share all joys and burdens, all victories and difficulties. I want us to inspire and encourage each other's writings.

Evelyn (*impatiently freeing himself*) All right! All right! There's no need to get maudlin about it. (*He smiles*) You know, this is the best thing that could have happened.

Oscar How can it be?

Evelyn He has gone too far this time. He has delivered himself into our hands.

Oscar What do you propose?

Evelyn Isn't it obvious? We'll take action at once.

Oscar Shouldn't we first...

Evelyn We'll put him in the dock at the Old Bailey. (*He pockets the card*) I'll go into the witness box and I'll tell the judge about his infamous conduct to my mother and to the rest of the family. My evidence will send him where he belongs—to prison.

Oscar But how can we be sure of that? What if we fail?

Evelyn How can we? He's libelled you, hasn't he? *And* published it in his own handwriting. I've always hoped that, one day, he would do something like this but never dreamed he'd go so far. I tell you we'll never get a better chance—never in a lifetime. We must start proceedings at once.

Oscar Wouldn't it perhaps be better...?

Evelyn What's the matter, Oscar? You're not afraid, are you?

Oscar Not exactly. It's just that I don't like going to law and I feel it would be better to avoid...

Evelyn There's no possible alternative. Now, with one blow, I can avenge all the injuries and insults which this horrible, unnatural man has inflicted on me and mine. Come on, Oscar. What are you waiting for? (*He begins to move away*) We must go to the solicitors at once.

Act I   21

Oscar Must go? Ought we not to consider...

But Evelyn has gone

Evelyn (*off*) Come along, Oscar. There's no time to lose.
Oscar Oh, very well. But I can't help feeling that we're being too precipitate.

Reluctantly, Oscar follows Evelyn

The platform is briefly empty

Then, from the opposite side from which he departed, Evelyn re-appears. He is now wearing spectacles and is carrying a brief—several thicknesses of large-size paper fastened by a pink ribbon

He sits at the table, unfastens the tape, and studies the brief. Doubtfully, he shakes his head and pushes the brief from him. He is deep in contemplation, chin in hand

Oscar enters

Evelyn Ah, Mr Wilde, do come in. I've been studying this case in some detail and I feel I ought to warn you.
Oscar Warn me, Sir Edward?
Evelyn Yes, there are several doubtful features and I would be failing in my duty if I didn't point them out.
Oscar Perhaps you will be more specific, Sir Edward.
Evelyn You are, it seems to me, in a position of some difficulty: a British jury is bound to sympathise with a father who has reason to object to his son's close association with an older man—an association which he considers unhealthy.
Oscar But there can be no possible reasons for his objections. None whatsoever.
Evelyn It is on that very point that I seek reassurance. (*He taps the brief*) I can only accept this brief, Mr Wilde, if you can assure me, on your word of honour as an English gentleman, that there is not, and never has been, any foundation for the charges laid against you.

Oscar draws himself erect and becomes, before our eyes, a pillar of probity

Oscar I can assure you, Sir Edward, on my word of honour as an English gentleman, that these charges are completely false from first to last.

As Oscar moves away and turns to us, Evelyn rifles through the brief

(*Confidentially*) I am, of course, by nature, temperament, sympathy and birth ... entirely Irish.

Evelyn gathers the brief together and looks up

Evelyn Then we have an excellent chance of worsting the Marquis. I thought, however, that I ought to issue a note of warning. Good day, Mr Wilde.
Oscar Good day, Sir Edward.

With the brief under his arm, Evelyn departs

Oscar gazes after him with a thoughtful expression

Penelope enters behind him. She is carrying her notebook and pencil

Penelope Mr Wilde.
Oscar (*alarmed*) Yes, yes. What is it? (*He turns and sees her*) Ah, it's you again. What is it this time, Miss Garland?
Penelope It's my readers, Mr Wilde. They are most interested...
Oscar Surely not in my play?
Penelope Not on this occasion. They're really interested in this court case in which you are involved.
Oscar Indeed?
Penelope Yes. They would like to know what are your thoughts at this time.
Oscar My thoughts at this time. (*He considers for a moment*) I place my faith in the British jury's sense of fair play...
Penelope (*writing busily*) "...British jury's senses of fair play".
Oscar (*turning away from her*) ...and in its monumental twelve-fold stupidity.
Penelope Thank you, Mr Wilde, and good luck.
Oscar Thank you. Most kind. I feel I am going to need it.

Penelope goes

Luck was not with me. The Marquis's hired detectives explored every crevice of my supposedly secret life. They produced in the witness box the companions of my revels and I was compelled to agree with Frank Harris. In the light of day, they did not in the least resemble panthers. They were sheepish, debauched clowns—and they sounded worse than they looked. The Marquis proved his allegations and won his case.

A Newsboy runs across the platform carrying his bag and bearing a bill upon which is printed the headline news which he proclaims

Act I 23

Newsboy Lord Queensberry Not Guilty! Oscar Wilde Loses Libel Case! Lord Queensberry Not Guilty!
Oscar So much for Bosie's threat to put his father in prison. Now, thanks to him, I stood to face the Law's most terrible revenge. Oh, I could have run away. Even the authorities encouraged me, gave me time to go. There were those in high places who wished to avoid the certain scandal. But, while I hesitated, while I debated...

The Newsboy runs on again. This time he has a different bill and cry

Newsboy Queensberry Case Sensation! Oscar Wilde Arrested! Oscar Wilde Arrested!
Oscar I was in prison, dazed by the sudden transition: one moment, it seemed, I was the most successful playwright of my generation, the darling of the drawing rooms, the toast of the Café Royal...

During the following, Evelyn enters and makes his way to the table previously occupied by Penelope. He is now wearing a barrister's wig and gown. He is carrying a brief

Next, I was alone in a dark cell, a prey to fear and guilt. Then came the two trials with my life proclaimed abominable and subjected to the public gaze.

Evelyn places the brief on the table. Then he sits and studies the brief

A loud doom-laden Voice calls out off stage

Voice Oscar Fingal O'Flahertie Wills Wilde how say you in answer to these charges against the peace of our sovereign Lady, the Queen, her Crown and dignity?
Oscar Not Guilty.

Evelyn rises and he and Oscar turn to face one another. Evelyn glances at his brief from time to time in the course of the following examination

Evelyn Have you ever adored a young man madly?
Oscar I have never adored anybody ... except myself.

There is some laughter and Oscar, encouraged, grows increasingly confident

Evelyn (*reading from his brief*) "Your soul walks between passion and poetry." (*He looks up*) Is that a beautiful line?
Oscar Not as you read it. You read it very badly.

Evelyn Is Park Walk about ten minutes walk from Tite Street?
Oscar I don't know. I never walk.
Evelyn And this boy at Worthing—you bought for him a suit of clothes, a silver-headed cane and a hat with bright ribbon?
Oscar That was his unfortunate choice.
Evelyn Did you know that he sold newspapers for a living?
Oscar This is the first time I have heard of his connection with literature.
Evelyn It was your custom to buy champagne for these young men. Do you drink champagne yourself?
Oscar Iced champagne is a favourite drink of—strictly against doctor's orders.
Evelyn (*indignantly*) Never mind your doctor's orders, sir!
Oscar (*mildly*) I never do.

There is an immediate outbreak of laughter and the Voice calls

Voice Silence! Silence in Court!

There is silence

Evelyn What enjoyment was it for you to entertain grooms and coachmen?
Oscar I have a passion to civilise the community.
Evelyn And this young man, Grainger—did you ever kiss him?
Oscar (*smiling*) Oh, dear, no. He was particularly plain. He was, unfortunately, particularly ugly. I pitied him for it.
Evelyn (*pouncing*) Was that the reason why you did not kiss him?

There is an echo effect which repeats "Was that the reason... Was that the reason why you did not kiss him?"

Oscar (*confused*) No, no... I... that was not the reason... You are confusing me... I did not mean...
Evelyn What is "the love that dare not speak its name"?

Having asked the question, Evelyn gathers up his brief and departs

Oscar has now regained his self-control

Oscar "The love that dare not speak its name" in this century is such affection of an elder for a younger man as there was between David and Jonathan, such as Plato made the very basis of his philosophy, and such as you find in the sonnets of Michelangelo and Shakespeare. It dictates and pervades great works of art like those of Shakespeare and Michelangelo and those two letters of mine, such as they are. It is in this century misunderstood, so

Act I

much misunderstood, that it may be described as "the love that dare not speak its name" and on account of it I am placed where I stand now. It is beautiful, it is fine, it is the noblest form of affection. There is nothing unnatural about it. It is intellectual and repeatedly exists between a younger and elder man, when the elder has the intellect and the younger man has all the joy, hope and glamour before him. That it should be so the world does not understand. The world mocks at it and sometimes one is put in the pillory for it.

There is an outburst of applause which is quelled by the Voice calling

Voice Silence! Silence in Court!

In the prevailing silence, Evelyn enters. He is now wearing the full-bottomed wig of a judge and appears most dignified

He bows stiffly and seats himself behind the central table

Evelyn Do you find the prisoner at the bar guilty or not guilty of the charges laid against him?
Voice Guilty.
Evelyn And that is the verdict of you all?
Voice It is.

The general lighting is now blacked out and Evelyn and Oscar are spotlit

Evelyn The crime of which you have been convicted is so bad that one has to put some restraint upon oneself from describing in language I would rather not use, the sentiments which must rise to the breast of every man of honour who has heard the details of these two terrible trials. That the jury has arrived at a correct verdict in this case, I cannot persuade myself to entertain a shadow of a doubt. It is the worst case I have ever tried. I shall, in the circumstances, be expected to pass the severest sentence the law allows. In my judgement, it is totally inadequate. The sentence of this Court is that you be imprisoned and kept to hard labour for two years.

The spot on Evelyn goes out

Oscar And I, my Lord? May I say nothing?

The spot on Oscar goes out and, from the darkness, echo answers him "Nothing... Nothing... Nothing..."

Act I ends in silence and darkness

ACT II

The setting is the same though now the central table may be regarded as the Governor's office and the single table and chair on the right represent Oscar's cell. There are papers, an inkstand and pen, a bundle of tracts and a clipboard on the central table. On the side table is a paper bag containing a pork pie and under the table is a chamber pot

As the CURTAIN *rises, Oscar is standing in front of the central table. He is wearing the broad-arrowed uniform and cap of a Victorian convict*

Oscar Prison. It is a word. It is a sentence spelling degradation, stupefaction and terror. But I had not plumbed the pit of humiliation until the day I stood with other convicts on the central platform of Clapham Junction Railway Station.

Background noises are heard throughout the rest of this scene: train whistles, engines shunting, carriage doors slamming, trains arriving and departing

You are to imagine that I was handcuffed so that I stood defenceless before a hostile world. (*He clasps his hands together and stands in the hunched attitude of a handcuffed man*) The more cruel of the passengers—which is to say the majority—jeered at us. There was one man I shall remember for the rest of my days...

Evelyn (*off*) My God! Look there! It's Oscar Wilde! Here, watch me!

Evelyn, disguised as a member of the labouring class, comes on

He pauses and looks back as if seeking the approval of his friends

Now watch... Just you watch me! (*He goes up boldly to Oscar and stands directly in front of him*) I know who you are. You're Oscar Wilde and this is what I think of you! (*He spits in Oscar's face*)

Oscar recoils. Laughing, Evelyn turns again to his friends

Did you see that? Did you see it? That's what I think of him!

Act II

Laughing, pleased with himself, Evelyn goes off

Dejectedly, Oscar lowers his head. There is brief silence. Then Oscar raises his head and looks about him with obvious distaste

Oscar If this is the way Queen Victoria treats her convicts, she doesn't deserve to have any.

A final shriek of the train whistle ends the train noises and the scene. Oscar unclasps his hands and rubs them to restore the circulation

I hope you will understand when I tell you that, for six months, I wept at that same hour every day and for the same space of time. Prison. It is a word echoing down the chill corridors and resounding in cells where weary men lie wakeful and utterly hopeless. But why should I attempt to describe prison to you in prose? Most of you know that I have written a poem, *The Ballad of Reading Gaol*, about my experiences in prison. There is one verse which truly reflects the sense of confinement, the depths of suffering:

> With midnight always in one's heart,
> And twilight in one's cell,
> We turn the crank, or tear the rope,
> Each in his separate Hell,
> And the silence is more awful far
> Than the sound of a brazen bell.

He stands for a moment staring bleakly before him, obviously affected by his recollections

But, even here, acts of kindness intrude. (*He goes over to the side table and takes up the paper bag*) This is the gift of a screw—warder to you—and I understand that it is edible... (*diffidently he peers inside the bag*) but I find it hard to believe. Mine is a shared condition and I have made several friends among my fellow prisoners. One of my particular friends is Davey Cross who may be best described as a simple-minded rapist with some talent as a gardener.

Evelyn shuffles on in the character of Davey Cross

Oscar Hallo, Davey.
Evelyn Hallo, Oscar. I been working in the Governor's garden.
Oscar Good for you. Who was the new man walking today with the Trial Men?
Evelyn Oh, him? Name of Wooldridge. He's a soldier. Killed his wife, he did.

Oscar Whatever for?
Evelyn Because he loved her.
Oscar That doesn't seem to be a good reason for killing her.
Evelyn Well, he did catch her with another bloke, didn't he? Anyway, he's got to swing.
Oscar He has?
Evelyn Sure as Gospel. He'll have to take the Eight O'clock Walk.
Oscar What's that?
Evelyn You don't know?

Oscar shakes his head

That's when they do it—at eight o'clock in that black shed in the yard.
Oscar I thought that was where they took the prisoners' photographs.
Evelyn (*losing interest*) I like working in gardens. (*Then, his face clouding*) It was in a garden where it happened.
Oscar If the Bible is to be believed, all our troubles started in a garden.
Evelyn I was weeding and this girl came up and ast me.
Oscar Asked you?
Evelyn Yes. She ast me and ast me to do it. She kept on asting me. But I wouldn't do it—not at first.
Oscar Quite right, too.
Evelyn When I did do it, she started shouting. People came and they brought me here.
Oscar You can't trust women, Davey.
Evelyn That's a fact. (*He looks pointedly at the paper bag*) What you got there, Oscar?
Oscar It's actually a gift from one of the staff. (*He peers doubtfully into the bag*) I have it on good authority that it is a pork pie, but I'm not altogether sure what to do with it.
Evelyn Not sure? (*He laughs*) You eat it, Oscar—that's what.
Oscar I don't think I'd care to. Would you ... would you like it?
Evelyn I would that. Give it here.

Oscar proffers the bag. Evelyn fairly snatches it from him, takes out the pie and drops the bag on the floor. He procedes to devour the pie watched by Oscar with absorbed interest

Oscar Is it all right?
Evelyn (*nodding and speaking with his mouth full*) Beautiful!
Oscar Hardly how I would have described it—but each according to his taste.

Anxiously he watches the other's obvious enjoyment of the pie

Act II 29

Don't let anyone see you eat it.
Evelyn (*cramming the last of the pie into his mouth*) All gone!

And so is Evelyn for he leaves with Oscar watching his departure

Then Oscar turns back to us

Oscar Then there is Fingers Bennett who seems likely to be another friend. (*Confidentially*) He is a very talented dip—pickpocket to you. In chapel he told me how he has had a most successful day at Lewes Races. He was tempted to make one last collection—his word. Well, it seemed that his intended victim turned out to be a police inspector who had had him under observation for some time. What struck Fingers as particularly unjust was that the inspector wasn't even on duty at the time but was present in his private capacity. I was sorry when Chapel was over—he seemed to have so much more to tell me.

Evelyn is now back in a very different character: a sharp-witted, darting-eyed, occasionally furtive Cockney

Oscar is just picking up the discarded paper bag as Evelyn, after glancing to left and right, calls out

Evelyn Whist, Oscar!

Startled, Oscar spins round and is greatly relieved when he sees Evelyn. He stows the paper bag inside his tunic

Oscar You scared me out of my wits, Fingers.
Evelyn (*with another glance to left and right*) I was there, Oscar.
Oscar There, dear boy?
Evelyn (*drawing himself up proudly*) I was there at the first night of *The Importance of Being Earnest*.
Oscar (*kindling*) You were? Were you really? (*Smiling, he regards Evelyn fondly*) Wasn't it the most glittering occasion? Was there ever an audience at once so distinguished and so responsive? And you were there at the St. James's Theatre that night...
Evelyn (*echoing Oscar's excitement*) I was there. In the Dress Circle.
Oscar In the Dress Circle... Oh, wasn't it one of the most splendid evenings ever? The witty speeches—for which I take full responsibility—the amusing situations—all my own work—with the bewitched audience hanging on every word. The music of the laughter and then that thunder of applause at the end.

Evelyn Oh, I didn't wait until then.
Oscar Didn't wait? You left?
Evelyn In the interval between Act One and Two.
Oscar (*puzzled*) But why? Were you bored?
Evelyn No, no. But I couldn't hang about. You see, I was loaded.
Oscar Loaded? You were loaded?
Evelyn I was that. I'd been busy. In my pockets I had (*he counts on his fingers*) five fob watches, seven wallets, three sovereign purses, four tie pins, two brooches and a necklace. (*He nods*) You're right, Oscar. It was what you might call a glittering occasion.

Evelyn nods again and goes out

Oscar gazes after him with admiration. He proceeds to count on his fingers

Oscar Four—no, five—fob watches, seven wallets, three sovereign purses, four tie pins, two brooches and a necklace. What an artist!

It grows darker on the platform

Prison—it is a prohibition, a denial, embracing rules, regulations, restrictions—so many of them that, through fear and ignorance, I broke many of them with distressful consequences. There was the time when we were exercising in the prison yard...

It is dark now except for the spot on Oscar

...and the prisoner behind me said...
Voice It is worse for a man such as you to endure all this.
Oscar No, my friend. We all suffer equally.
Voice Those two men! C-3-3 and C-6-7! On report for talking!

Evelyn has entered during the darkness and now, as the Light comes up, is seen to be seated at the central table in the role of Major Isaacson, the Prison Governor

Evelyn (*testily*) All right. I'll see the next one. (*He consults a paper on the table*) C-3-3.

Oscar turns towards him and moves over to the central table

Oh, it's Wilde. Wilde again.
Oscar As you say, sir, Wilde again. (*He has, most untidily, attempted the position of attention*)

Act II

Evelyn At ease, man. At ease.

Oscar relaxes

What is the matter with you, Wilde? Why are you always breaking regulations?
Oscar What is the matter with me? Sheer ignorance, sir.
Evelyn Ignorance? I don't understand you.
Oscar That, sir, is a large part of my trouble.
Evelyn (*ominously*) Are you, perhaps, trying to be funny at my expense?
Oscar Oh no, sir. It is just that there are too many regulations.
Evelyn Too many?
Oscar Far too many, sir. Why isn't it possible to keep them to a small, tidy number like the Ten Commandments?
Evelyn Very well. V-e-r-y well. We'll deal with this latest transgression. The Duty Officer reports that you spoke to another prisoner (*he consults his paper*) during exercise contrary to regulations.
Oscar That is quite true, sir. The Duty Officer's report is correct.
Evelyn Thank you for the confirmation. You realize, of course, that the prisoner who began the conversation automatically renders himself liable to fourteen days' solitary confinement? The prisoner who answers renders himself liable to seven days' solitary confinement.
Oscar Yes. I was aware of the penalty, sir.
Evelyn What have you to say for yourself? Who spoke first?
Oscar Oh, I did, sir.
Evelyn You did, did you?
Oscar I made some trivial observation—passed the time of day.
Evelyn Now listen to me very carefully. Because of your regrettable tendencies, I have to be especially vigilant in order to protect the other prisoners under my care. Once again, Wilde, I award you fourteen days' solitary confinement.
Oscar I never expected less, sir.
Evelyn Then I am pleased not to disappoint you. It is now my pleasant duty to inform you that, as a result of your continued disregard of regulations, you have now forfeited any prospect you might have had of obtaining remission of your sentence.

Stricken, Oscar stares at him

Do you understand, Wilde? You will now have to serve your full sentence.
Oscar I do understand, sir.
Evelyn The longer you are here, Wilde, the greater is the possibility of you being cured of your unnatural tendencies. Here you are being subjected to

something you have hitherto lacked—discipline. I am a great believer in discipline, Wilde.
Oscar That, sir, is all too evident.
Evelyn Now, before you leave to begin your sentence, you may be interested to learn that the other prisoner admitted that it was he who began the conversation in the yard. So you see that your ridiculous attempt to take the blame upon yourself has been quite useless. I have also awarded the other prisoner fourteen days' solitary confinement.
Oscar Sir, I congratulate you. Yours is the Judgement of Solomon—in reverse. By your leave, sir... (*He walks away in the direction of the other table*)
Evelyn (*shouting*) Take that man away to solitary!

The Light is fading and Evelyn repeats in an effort to understand the words

The Judgement of Solomon...

The scene blacks out briefly. When the Light comes up to full, Oscar has moved the chair from behind the side table. He has turned the chair so that its back is to the audience and he straddles it. In the meantime, Evelyn, in the guise of the Chaplain, has gathered the bundle of tracts from the central table

Oscar If you were a prisoner here, you would, in this terrible situation, look to the prison chaplains for succour and comfort. You would look in vain. As a body, they are entirely useless. As a class, they are well-meaning but foolish, indeed, silly men who are no help to the unfortunates in their spiritual care. Once every six weeks the chaplain visits the prisoner in his cell.
Voice Stand by C-3-3! Stand by for the Chaplain's visit!

With the bundle of tracts in his hand, Evelyn approaches Oscar. Oscar rises and stands at attention in anticipation of the visit... Evelyn approaches him

Evelyn Good evening.
Oscar (*listlessly*) Is it evening? (*He relaxes*) I didn't know what time of day it was. (*Suddenly recollecting*) Did you know, sir, that a man is to be killed in this prison—killed with all the barbarity that the Law allows at eight o'clock tomorrow morning?
Evelyn If you mean the convicted murderer, I did know. I shall, in his case, be doing my best to prepare him to meet his God and reconcile him to his fate.
Oscar With respect, sir, I think you will fail in both endeavours.
Evelyn My immediate concern is your state of mind. Are you more reconciled than you were at the time of my last visit?

Act II

Oscar Patience is a virtue and therefore has no place here. Apathy is what one needs in the face of despair but apathy is a vice and I have enough of those—more than enough as you will be the first to admit.
Evelyn Has your situation improved since my last visit?
Oscar Improved? How can it ever improve? I am ruined professionally, my children no longer bear my name and I have lost every stick and stone I possessed.
Evelyn Yes, you told me. You have suffered a great deal.
Oscar There is more. Since I saw you, I have been declared bankrupt because those who promised to pay my costs have gone back on their word. Perhaps you would recommend that I should pray for these ... defaulters.
Evelyn It might help if you forgave them. Surely, there is some ray of light in all this darkness.
Oscar None. Just gloom impenetrable ... and yet...
Evelyn Yes?
Oscar There is just one thing—my wife has agreed not to divorce me.
Evelyn Then you have reason to be grateful.
Oscar But she says nothing about setting up home together when I am released.
Evelyn That is something for which you must work and pray.
Oscar If you will forgive me for saying so, sir, you are like a quack doctor— you have only one remedy for all diseases. I have been thinking a good deal since your last visit. Religiously, in a sense.
Evelyn (*suspiciously*) Indeed?
Oscar Yes. All these multitudinous sorrows crowding in upon me. I have never, in my life, seen a man so suddenly and disastrously afflicted. I have tried, without success, to find a parallel in history.
Evelyn You have certainly had a great deal to bear. But some of the blessed saints...
Oscar You anticipate me, reverend sir. Could it be, do you think, that God is testing and trying my spirit with the intention of making me a saint?
Evelyn (*deeply shocked*) Mr Wilde! You would have to change beyond all knowledge before you became a good man and then you would have to change out of all recognition before you became a saint.
Oscar The trouble with you, sir, is that, like most priests, you don't really believe in miracles.
Evelyn I'll leave you, Mr Wilde. (*He thrusts a tract into Oscar's reluctant hand*) Here, take this tract. Digest it and it will give you a more reasonable view of life.
Oscar I have never sought a reasonable view of life. Surely, that is for shopkeepers and insurance brokers. Do you believe that the prisons of this country might be improved?
Evelyn (*cautiously*) No doubt there is room for considerable improvement.

Oscar I think we might begin by humanising the prison governors. Then we might try to civilise the warders and, lastly, we might attempt to Christianise the chaplains.

Evelyn gives him a hard, long stare, turns and begins to walk away. Then he pauses and turns again to Oscar

Evelyn Mr Wilde, did you have family prayers in your home?
Oscar No, I am afraid not.
Evelyn You see where you are now.

He accords Oscar a dismissive nod and goes, leaving Oscar staring after him. Then Oscar tears up the tract and places the pieces on the side table. Evelyn sits at the central table where he rids himself of the remaining tracts. Oscar turns again to the audience

Oscar The night before a prisoner is executed, the prison becomes a sounding board of terror, of apprehension and mortal dread.

Evelyn rises

To the prisoners, locked in their darkened cells, the tension is unbearable.

Now Evelyn and Oscar stand facing the audience as the platform darkens until the only Light is provided by the two spotlights which illuminate them both. There is a sudden loud clanking noise as somebody strikes a pipe with a piece of metal

Evelyn Are you there, Oscar?
Oscar Of course I'm here, Fingers. Where else should I be?
Evelyn How is he, do you think? How is Wooldridge?
Oscar How would you be in his place?
Evelyn Frightened to death. What is he doing now, do you think?
Oscar He's lying there in the condemned cell, sleeping, waking, sleeping again, dreaming, remembering ... wasting away what little time is left to him.
Evelyn Yes, that's the way it is.
Oscar Listen now and you can hear his life ticking away ... ticking away...

And, as they listen, the ticking of a clock is suddenly audible. Then it fades

Evelyn The screws stand there waiting ... and they know.
Oscar What do they know?

Act II 35

Evelyn They know what it's like to kill a man. They know the Governor will come along to make it official. Then comes the Chaplain to bless the occasion and he'll mumble the words...
Oscar The words that bring no comfort ... no hope.
Evelyn True enough. True enough.
Oscar You've seen it all before, Fingers.
Evelyn Three times, Oscar. I know how it'll be. They'll pinion him, take him by the arm and thrust him up the few steps to the trap.
Oscar No! No!

Hereafter, Oscar listens in fascinated horror

Evelyn They'll push him, quite gently, on to the trap. The hangman will adjust the noose—quite firmly—with the knot just where it will do most good. And then ... then they'll spring the trap!
Oscar Please God, NO!
Evelyn He spins ... spins ... and strangles in the agony of violent death.
Oscar I don't want to hear. (*He covers his ears*) Stop it! Stop it!
Evelyn (*unheeding*) Face livid, eyeballs protruding, blackened lips drawn back in protest!
Oscar (*shrieking*) I won't listen! I won't listen!

His voice is drowned by a great outbreak of noise as the prisoners express their protest by beating upon the walls with their utensils. The spot goes out on Evelyn. The prisoners' clamour dies away abruptly as the prison clock slowly strikes eight

Evelyn (*from the darkness*) It's over. He's gone.
Oscar Murderers! Killers! Bloody murderers. (*He weeps*) Help me! Oh, God, help me! (*Then he raises his head and looks directly at the audience*) But there was no help. None for him. None for me. He was shrouded in quicklime and buried in an unhallowed grave. He had no requiem but I wrote his epitaph in that same poem—*The Ballad of Reading Gaol*.
        Yet all is well; he has but passed
        To Life's appointed bourne:
        And alien tears will fill for him
        Pity's long-broken urn,
        For his mourners will be outcast men
        And outcasts always mourn.
Let that serve as passing bell for all us outcasts.

The spot goes out on Oscar and there is total darkness during which Evelyn picks up the clipboard. When the Light comes up again, Oscar is sitting at the side table. A Voice calls loudly

Voice Come on! Get slopped out! Get them emptied! Empty those chamber pots!

Confused, Oscar rises

That means you, C-3-3!
Oscar Oh, yes! At once!

He rummages under the table, produces the chamber pot and has just regained the perpendicular when the Voice is heard again

Voice Stand by C-3-3! Stand by for the Governor's visit!

Oscar stands irresolute holding the chamber pot and he comes slowly, sloppily, to the position of attention

Evelyn enters in the character of the new Governor, Major Nelson. He is carrying the clipboard

Evelyn Good morning, Wilde.
Oscar You're not ... not...
Evelyn Oh yes, I am. I am the Governor—the new Governor. My name is Nelson—Major Nelson. I took over yesterday afternoon and I have availed myself of the first opportunity to come and see the most distinguished of my charges. (*He steps back a pace, wrinkles his nose, waves his free hand and regards the chamber pot with some distaste*) Do you think you could get rid of that ... thing for a few minutes?
Oscar Oh, yes ... yes. Right away, sir! (*Hurriedly, he restores the offending chamber pot to its former resting place under the table. Then he resumes his former posture*)
Evelyn Please stand at ease. That is if you are supposed to be standing at attention.
Oscar (*relaxing*) It is very difficult to tell, sir. Part of the trouble is these clothes. They are quite unable to come to attention and it is not a position I find natural to me.
Evelyn That I can readily appreciate. There is another reason why I was so anxious to make your acquaintance. Did you know that the correspondence about you has assumed such proportions that you have a large, thick file to yourself?
Oscar I am not in the least surprised, sir.
Evelyn Also, I heard a great deal about you from Major Isaacson.
Oscar I'm sure you did, sir.
Evelyn Nothing he said will influence me. I form my own impressions. One

Act II 37

of my first duties has been to study the somewhat extended letter you have been writing to Lord Alfred Douglas over these past weeks.

Oscar reacts

Oh, don't be alarmed, Wilde. Although the pages are taken from you as a matter of routine, at the end of each day, they are in safekeeping. I have to read what you write as part of my official duty.
Oscar Will the letter be returned to me, sir?
Evelyn Most certainly it will—when you are released. But, speaking for myself... (*He breaks off*) Never mind. May I say that I am pleased you are writing again—whatever the subject.
Oscar Thank you, sir.
Evelyn My visit this morning, however, is primarily concerned with your work for Her Majesty's Government.
Oscar Oh, dear!
Evelyn (*consulting a paper held by the clipboard*) Your work, as recorded here, has been something less than satisfactory. For instance, you rarely seem to have fulfilled your quota of oakum picking.
Oscar I am sorry, sir, but it was not a task to which I could give my mind.
Evelyn That is understandable. Oakum picking is not intended to be mentally stimulating.
Oscar I wish you could tell me its purpose, sir.
Evelyn It has no real purpose—it is merely a time-wasting occupation. (*Again, he studies the clipboard in his hand*) Then I see that you were put to bookbinding.
Oscar (*shaking his head*) That was one of Major Isaacson's less happy inspirations. He was so naïve that he thought a writer would know how to bind books. As well expect a musician to construct a piano. No. Bookbinding calls for a degree of manual dexterity which I do not possess. Indeed, in such matters, I have a degree of natural clumsiness so remarkable that it amounts almost to a gift.
Evelyn Have you? Have you, indeed? You pose a problem, Wilde. I look at this (*he indicates the clipboard*) and I look at you. Then I ask myself, "What am I to do with him?"
Oscar (*nodding sympathetically*) I can see that there is a problem. I sympathise with you in your dilemma, sir.
Evelyn There is a job I have in mind for you.
Oscar (*encouraging*) Yes, sir...
Evelyn Would you care to be the schoolmaster's orderly?
Oscar What would be my duties, sir?
Evelyn Well, they would not involve any degree of manual dexterity.
Oscar I am relieved to hear it.

Evelyn In fact, they would be purely nominal. But you would have charge of the library.
Oscar (*kindling*) The library?!
Evelyn Do you find the proposal attractive?
Oscar I cannot tell you how attractive, sir.
Evelyn Then perhaps we can discuss the matter in my office this afternoon.
Oscar Your office?
Evelyn Have you any objection?
Oscar No ... no. It is just that all my previous visits to the Governor's office have been for the purpose of receiving punishment.
Evelyn This time it will be different. (*He is about to leave but turns again to Oscar*) I have something to ask you, but perhaps the question is indiscreet so early in our acquaintance.
Oscar Questions are never indiscreet, sir. Answers sometimes are.
Evelyn Very well. Although I said I was pleased that you are writing this marathon letter to Lord Alfred Douglas, I feel bound to ask: why do you find it necessary to revive so much unhappiness and anguish? It is unworthy of you.
Oscar I am deeply touched that you should think so. It is as the result of an action forced upon me by Lord Alfred that I find myself here. The letter is something I must write for his sake as well as my own.
Evelyn You deceive yourself. This letter is full of venom and overflowing with self-pity. Write it if you must and then tear it up. That, I assure you, would be best for all concerned.

As Oscar seems about to speak, Evelyn raises his hand

No, no. Please don't say anything. Think about it.
Oscar Yes, sir. I'll do as you say. But I don't expect to change my mind. I would be going against my nature.
Evelyn But, surely, that is what you have been doing for this long time past.

Evelyn nods to Oscar and goes out briskly

Oscar stands deep in thought but he is shaken out of his musing when the Voice calls out

Voice Get moving there, C-3-3! Let's have that chamber pot emptied or you'll be on Report!
Oscar Yes, yes. Right away!

He stoops, collects the chamber pot from under the table as the Voice calls again

Act II

Voice Come on, C-3-3! You're late! What's keeping you?
Oscar (*panicking*) I'm coming! I'm coming at once!

Oscar scurries off with the chamber pot

From the other entrance, Evelyn enters in the character of Martin, the warder

There is an outbreak of bird-song to indicate that this scene is out-of-doors. Evelyn looks behind him and calls

Evelyn Come on, now. We haven't got all day! (*He grows increasingly impatient and shouts*) And pick up that hoe! You're going to need it!

Oscar comes in carrying a hoe

He breathes deeply and looks about him with approval

Oscar I never thought that a time would come when I would actually appreciate fresh air.
Evelyn (*indicating*) He wants those deck chairs moved. Just give me a hand.

They move the chairs so that they are facing the audience

That's where he wants them. Now you'd better get started on the weeding right away, Mr Wilde.
Oscar Yes, of course. Right away. (*He leans on the hoe*) You know, it never struck me that a warder might be interested in literature.
Evelyn I've always been a great reader.
Oscar Have you now? I'm very glad to hear it. What does Bacon say? "Reading maketh a full man."
Evelyn Does he, sir? Now which Bacon is that? Would it be the one called Fat Bacon? The one we had in here?
Oscar I shouldn't think so. He was, in fact, before your time.
Evelyn I keep reading, Mr Wilde, and I don't know whether I'm on the right track ... whether I'm reading the proper authors...
Oscar (*deeply concerned*) My dear fellow, we can't have you tormented by doubt. Here, let us sit down here and have a literary discussion such as we might have at my club. (*He places the hoe on the ground, settles in one of the chairs and, with a graceful wave of the hand, invites the warder to sit down*)
Evelyn (*troubled*) No, no, we mustn't sit down here, Mr Wilde. After all, it's the Governor's garden and you're supposed to——

Oscar Now where's the harm? Just for a few minutes ... while we resolve your doubts. I promise you that I'll work twice as hard afterwards.

Evelyn (*with obvious reluctance*) All right then. Just for a few minutes. (*He sits in the other chair*)

Oscar Now consider yourself free to ask me anything. Anything at all.

Evelyn Well, Charles Dickens, sir. Would he be considered a great writer?

Oscar (*judicially*) Oh, yes. Unquestionably. You see, he is no longer alive. Death to a writer is what canonisation is to a martyr. It enhances him ... it hallows him.

Evelyn Does it indeed, sir?

Oscar Without a shadow of doubt. Why if Shakespeare were alive today, he would be accounted of little more consequence than ... than Bernard Shaw.

Evelyn Who is Bernard Shaw, Mr Wilde?

Oscar He is a writer of considerable talent. Make a note of the name.

Evelyn Yes, sir. Bernard Shaw. (*He looks troubled and tries to rise*)

Oscar shakes his head and motions him to relax. Reluctantly, Evelyn sinks back into his chair

Oscar What are you reading now?

Evelyn I've just finished reading *David Copperfield*. It's the tenth time I've read it.

Oscar What dogged determination!

Evelyn Now I'm reading *The Old Curiosity Shop*.

Oscar Doubtless for the tenth time.

Evelyn (*counting on his fingers*) No ... no. I believe I've only read it six times.

Oscar My dear man, you must persevere! Persevere! Do you like the book?

Evelyn (*rapt*) I love it! I love that book! Don't you love it, sir?

Oscar I do indeed. One would need to have a heart of stone to read of the death of Little Nell without laughing.

Evelyn It takes different people different ways—I always cry.

Oscar Your sentiments do you infinite credit.

Evelyn What do you think of Ouida, sir?

Oscar I try not to. If I find myself tempted, I just close my eyes and try counting sheep—much more beneficial.

Evelyn Then there's Mr Henry James—of course, he's an American.

Oscar That is so. He is an American, moreover, who is trying to assimilate the European climate of thought. In the circumstances, it should not surprise us that he writes fiction as if it were a painful duty.

Evelyn And what about Marie Corelli, sir? Would you consider her a great writer?

Act II

Oscar I am afraid not. (*He looks cautiously to left and right and then adds confidentially*) Don't think that I have anything against her character but, from the way she writes, she ought to be in here.
Evelyn (*awed*) You don't say, sir! You don't say! (*He rises*) It is very kind of you to spare me so much of your time.
Oscar Don't mention it. I have plenty of time, my dear fellow. Time to spare. Time to waste. Time to kill. I have enjoyed myself immensely.

Evelyn rises and picks up the hoe

Evelyn Oh, I almost forgot. I am a great admirer of Mr George Meredith. Where would you place him, Mr Wilde?
Oscar Meredith... Meredith I consider to be a prose Browning...
Evelyn (*nodding*) "A prose Browning..."
Oscar And so is Browning.

Puzzled, Evelyn moves away. Then he pauses, to echo

Evelyn "...And so is Browning." (*Completely bewildered, he shakes his head. Then he becomes aware of the hoe in his hand*) Here, come on! You ought to have this!

Oscar rises and Evelyn thrusts the hoe into his reluctant hand

Go and get some weeding done. Start with that bed near the pear tree.

He sits down. Oscar contemplates him

Now do get a move on. If you don't, we'll both be in trouble.
Oscar It's all your fault.
Evelyn My fault?
Oscar You're such a *witty* listener.

Oscar goes

Evelyn settles back and, after a glance to right and left, produces a packet of cigarettes and a box of matches from his pocket. He lights up and inhales briefly

Oscar enters carrying a plant

Some of these weeds have grown enormously. Just look at this one.
Evelyn (*ominously*) Do you know what it is?

Oscar A weed... Isn't it?

Evelyn It's a flower. It's a columbine—or it would have been if you'd left it where it was.

Oscar Oh, dear! I've always bought flowers from shops or from women in the street. I've never really studied them in the raw.

Evelyn (*rising*) What do you mean—"in the raw".

Oscar Well... like this. I'm afraid I've pulled up about half a dozen and left them beside the path.

Evelyn Good God in Heaven! I'd better see what I can do.

Evelyn rushes off

Oscar watches him go but makes no attempt to follow him. Instead, he puts down the hoe and settles himself in one of the chairs as the sound of bird-song swells

Oscar This is the way to commune with Nature.

He tips his hat over his eyes and composes himself to slumber as the bird-song ceases and the Light goes out briefly

> *When it comes up to full again, Oscar and the hoe have gone. The chairs are back in place—one on either side of the central table. Evelyn is seated behind it. He rises to welcome Penelope who has apparently just been ushered into his office. She is again carrying the briefcase*

Evelyn Ah, Mrs Wilde! I am so glad to meet you.

Penelope But I was expecting...

Evelyn Major Isaacson, no doubt. I have recently replaced him. (*He takes her hand*) There have been a number of changes here—for the better, I like to think. Please sit down.

She does so and he follows her example

Penelope My husband ... is he well?

Evelyn I would say he is in better health and spirits than when you saw him last.

Penelope That is good news.

Evelyn And it will do him a power of good to see you—even in the unhappy circumstances.

Penelope I thought it better that I should...

Evelyn No doubt about it. You are absolutely right. Also it seems to me that your visit is timely when one considers that the day of his release draws

Act II 43

nearer. Today you will have opportunity to discuss your ... future arrangements.
Penelope That is what I had in mind.
Evelyn If I could just offer a word of advice...
Penelope Yes?
Evelyn Men in his situation are especially sensitive.
Penelope I do realize that.
Evelyn He will need all the understanding, all the sympathy and all the encouragement you can give him at this time. (*He smiles*) But I am preaching to the converted. You know just what to say, how to reassure him.
Penelope But we've only just met. How can you be so sure?
Evelyn In time one becomes something of a judge of character merely by sitting behind this desk. I consider Mr Wilde to be most fortunate to have you waiting for him when he is released. Mr Wilde will be here shortly— I thought it best, in the circumstances, for you to meet here in the office. (*He rises, comes round the desk and indicates his own chair*)

Penelope also rises

If you were to sit there, Mrs Wilde...

She takes his proffered hand

It has been a great pleasure to meet you, Mrs Wilde.
Penelope I am glad to have met you, Major Nelson.

Evelyn goes

Penelope sits in Evelyn's chair and looks about her fearfully

What a dreadful, dreadful place! (*She picks up her briefcase, opens it and, having reassured herself as to its contents, closes it and replaces it beside the chair*)

Oscar appears escorted by Evelyn who is now in the character of Prison Officer Tom Martin

Oscar halts when he sees Penelope

Oscar Constance!

Penelope rises

They only told me that it was a special visit.
Penelope How are you, Oscar?
Oscar Well enough.

Pause

All things considered.
Evelyn (*to Oscar*) Will you please sit down.

Oscar sits in the visitor's chair

You are both to remain seated throughout this interview. It is not permitted for the prisoner and the visitor to approach one another. (*To Penelope*) I have to be present, ma'am, but I will not interfere unless it should become necessary.
Penelope Thank you.

Hereafter, Evelyn stands at ease some little way from the central table and does not appear to take any interest in the following conversation

Oscar It's not the children?
Penelope No, they're all right. It's your mother.
Oscar Is she...?
Penelope She died, Oscar.
Oscar Oh, no! I didn't know she was ill. How did she die?
Penelope She caught a chill. It turned to bronchitis and there were complications. She asked for you. They wrote enquiring if you would be allowed to visit her but the reply, when it came, said it would not be possible.
Oscar (*stonily*) Not possible.
Penelope When they told your mother that you would not be allowed to come, she turned her face to the wall and said, "May the prison help him!"
Oscar Poor Mother! (*His expression changing*) Now I remember. I dreamed of her last night. It seemed that she came to me in my cell. She was wearing her hat and coat. I asked her to take them off. She shook her head sadly—and vanished. I woke, slept again and did not remember until now. It was very kind of you, Constance, to come all this way...
Penelope I didn't want you to hear it officially. I thought it would be better if I told you.
Oscar Oh, it is better. Incomparably better. You knew her—knew what she was to me. I shall find time to mourn her. You said the boys were well?
Penelope They're very well. They're growing, of course—especially Cyril.
Oscar And getting on at school?

Act II   45

Penelope Oh, yes. They're doing well.
Oscar Are they getting used to their new name?
Penelope As far as I can tell.
Oscar I think of you often, Constance. You have so great a responsibility in bringing up the boys.
Penelope And what am I to do, Oscar?
Oscar You must appoint a guardian for them—someone you can trust. Mothers are too indulgent, Constance. One has only to see what his mother has made of Bosie Douglas.
Penelope Bosie! Do we have to speak of him? Whenever I hear his ridiculous name, I feel sick at heart ... sick to death. I remember what he has done to you ... to both of us. I should have thought he would have been the last...
Oscar I'm truly sorry, my dear. I was merely citing Bosie as perhaps the worst example of a spoiled child. Perhaps he'll begin to realize it when he receives the letter I'm writing.
Penelope (*rising*) Letter? You're writing a letter to Bosie? What on earth for?
Oscar To show him how horribly he has betrayed our relationship. I want him to know the depth of my suffering, the completeness of my destruction.
Penelope If you have the time and the inclination to write, should you not write to me or to your sons so that they might one day arrive at an understanding of your actions? Bosie! When you speak of him, I feel angry... (*she sits again*) then sick and wretched.
Oscar So do I—and I have more time for dwelling on past misdeeds. But I know I must write to him.
Penelope You must do as you please. You say you often think of me but not, I'm sure, as often as I think of you. I try to reconcile what you told me when I was here before with our lives together ... with your genius as a writer. And I can't! I just can't!
Oscar I cannot excuse—I can only seek to explain it. What the paradox was to me in literature, I expressed as perversity in my life. It seems to me now ... inescapable. As an artist, I was impelled to fulfil my nature—every part of it.
Penelope (*bitterly*) Then I hope that the satisfaction of having fulfilled your nature compensates you for your misery and ours. If I have seemed harsh on you, Oscar, you must forgive me for I have had a great deal to bear in this past year.
Oscar (*weeping*) Oh, Constance, you are an angel and my conduct deserves the reproach—no, the condemnation—of angels. I hope a time will come when I shall be worthy of your kindness.
Penelope Do you think that time will ever come? Have we any hope of ever being together? Will you be different when you leave this place?
Oscar I think there is a very real chance of us being together again but our future depends upon you more than me. Of course I shall be different. I

shall be humbler, more compassionate. But not better—prison does not ennoble.

Penelope You don't answer the question. Are you afraid? Will ... will you live as you did before? Will you be like that again? If so, then...

Oscar How can I tell? It is like asking me how I shall conduct myself in the Hereafter.

Penelope (*rising*) Answer me! How are you resolved to live when you leave here?

Oscar As best I can. I ask myself your questions, Constance, and the answers I get are never the same—which suggests that I am a vacillating creature. This much I know: I have been true to my nature and it is for that I am being cruelly punished. In another time and another country, I would not have merited punishment.

Penelope It seems to me, Oscar, that you are almost beyond help. If you cannot see that you have done wrong and need to amend, then I can see no future for us.

Oscar My dear, I am what I am. I shall try to be what you would wish, but I fear there will be times——

Penelope Oh, no! If there was only myself to be considered... (*She sits again*) But there are the boys...

Oscar The boys...

Penelope You ask too much, Oscar. You must see that I could not possibly submit myself and the boys to the furtive horror of such an existence. Either you break completely with the past...

Oscar (*rising*) Or else? No need to complete the sentence. The verdict is in your face.

Evelyn The prisoner will remain seated.

Oscar Of course. (*He sits again*) You are both judge and jury and you have condemned me before I have committed any crime.

Penelope You are right to describe yourself as a lord of language. You can make words mean anything you choose. You can spin a web of words to show that you are blameless and prove the other person to be both stupid and guilty. But the spell has ceased to work on me. You have had your chance, Oscar.

Oscar Chance? (*He shakes his head*) It does not seem so to me. I have been condemned.

Penelope If you have, it is on your own evidence. I wonder if I have been wrong about you ... if I have always been wrong. Because I know what they say about me is true.

Oscar What do they say?

Penelope That I am soft-hearted ... stubborn ... hopelessly sentimental ... unwilling to see things as they are ... reluctant to appreciate what is before my face.

Oscar Who says this? Who?

Act II 47

Penelope My relatives—my advisers. They are clearly right about me. They could be right, too, when they say you must serve a probationary period before we live together again.
Oscar You cannot possibly agree with them. (*He watches her face for some sign that she will relent*)

There is none

But you do. Perhaps you will be kind enough to explain the terms of this probationary period.
Penelope Yes. A Deed of Arrangement has been drawn up. You are to receive one hundred and fifty pounds per annum as life interest in my marriage settlement. I am sorry it is so little but we are not rich ... and there are the boys.
Oscar I do understand. In my situation, I must be grateful for any mercies—however small. But I detect a certain hesitancy. The allowance is, perhaps, conditional?
Penelope Indeed it is. The Deed becomes void if you should be involved in any scandal or if it can be proved that you are consorting with any notoriously disreputable persons.

Furious, Oscar rises

Oscar Who are these people who think they can impose——
Evelyn (*topping him*) The prisoner will remain seated!

Oscar sits again

Penelope I have been asked to emphasise that Lord Alfred Douglas is certainly regarded as "a notoriously disreputable person".
Oscar These advisors of yours don't believe in mincing their words, do they? Is there more, Constance?
Penelope Yes, Oscar. (*She produces her briefcase, opens it and takes from it a document. Then she rises, crosses to Evelyn and gives him the document*) Would you please give this to Mr Wilde?
Evelyn (*after a quick glance at the Deed*) Certainly, Madam. (*He goes over to Oscar and hands the document to him*)

Oscar studies it and, while he is doing so, Penelope resumes her seat and Evelyn takes up his former position. At length, Oscar looks up from the paper in bewilderment

Oscar Do they really mean all this—that I am to sign away all right to my children, that I am to lose my sole income if I as much as write to Bosie?

Penelope Yes, Oscar.
Oscar Who is responsible for drawing up this ... this infamous document?
Penelope Oscar, my advisors have given instructions——
Oscar (*disgustedly*) Your advisors!
Penelope They stipulate this period of probation——
Oscar A period of probation! What do they think I am? Probationary period, indeed!

Penelope rises and makes a sign to Evelyn. With him preceding her, she moves as if to leave. From the exit, Penelope looks back. Oscar rises when he realizes that she is about to leave

Constance! Constance! Come back! Don't go! What do they think I am? You can't mean that you... (*He is near to weeping*) Constance! Oh, Constance!

But Penelope and Evelyn have gone

Oscar crumples the document in his hand and, infinitely dejected, he sits again. Then he smoothes out the document and reads

"A Deed of Arrangement..." (*He reads on*) Clauses ... sub-clauses ... prohibitions ... threats ... restrictions ... punishments ... and all in the name of justice and conformity. (*He attempts to read further but, defeated, casts the paper from him so that it lies on the table. Then he turns to address us directly*) Prison... Here is sanctuary from the unforgiving, a refuge from those who would shun me, a haven from the terrors and torments out there. (*His gesture indicates the world beyond the prison. He is sitting staring helplessly before him*)

Evelyn enters as Major Nelson and comes over to him

Evelyn I have just heard what happened. How are you?
Oscar As well as can be expected in the circumstances. I have been sitting here endeavouring to adjust to the knowledge that I am considered unfit company for my own children. (*He picks up the Deed and flourishes it*) And I have been trying, without success, to take in the full import of this piece of paper which legally separates me from my wife and children.
Evelyn I thought your wife was here on a mission of reconciliation.
Oscar If that was her intention, she managed to disguise it very well. (*He shakes his head*) I realize that I have already lived several lives having been student, poet, editor, playwright and prisoner. I have also been a son, a husband and a father. Each life ends in a little death and those lives are now behind me. The life I have now to lead is that of a pariah, an outcast.

Act II

Evelyn Understandably, you exaggerate. You need time to adjust to your situation. Others have done so.
Oscar With respect, they were not circumstanced as I am. I am shocked to discover that I do not wish to leave this place.
Evelyn In one way or another, you will survive. A year from now, you will marvel that you ever doubted.
Oscar Let us hope you are right. A year from now... (*Disconcerted, he breaks off and springs to his feet*) I have just realized, sir, that, contrary to all regulations, I am sitting in your presence.
Evelyn Oh, please sit down. (*He sits on the other side of the table*) Come now, you were saying that a year from now...
Oscar A year from now I see myself as shunned by all except my closest friends, (*he sits again*) dragging out my miserable existence with no means, no urge to write ... sponging on my friends ... begging from acquaintances. I see myself as becoming demanding, querulous, foolishly extravagant.
Evelyn If you see this...
Oscar I see and am powerless in the knowledge of my own nature for I have learned a good deal about myself in this place. I know myself to be totally amoral and wholly unstable.
Evelyn If you know all this, you can prepare safeguards, erect defences. You have remarkable qualities.
Oscar At the risk of embarrassing me, enumerate them.
Evelyn I'm not sure that I could ... off hand.
Oscar At least make the effort.
Evelyn Very well. Let me see... (*He considers*) You are capable of great application ... you are enormously talented, most eloquent, wonderfully witty, kind, generous and loyal to friends.
Oscar My dear sir! What an end-of-term report! Oh, if I could only be accepted again as a writer!
Evelyn I confidently prophesy that you will be not only accepted but acclaimed. (*He regards Oscar closely*) And you feel better now—easier in your mind?
Oscar When I am speaking to you like this, I am appreciably easier in my mind. It is when I am sitting alone in my cell...
Evelyn Then you must recall my catalogue of your qualities and my predictions for your future.
Oscar Oh, believe me, I am greatly comforted...
Evelyn There!
Oscar ...But not entirely convinced. (*Sensing that the interview is at an end, he rises*) Thank you, sir, for your good opinion.
Evelyn (*smiling*) Conduct the prisoner to his cell!

Oscar goes off

Evelyn turns to the audience

You'll agree that I did my best to help him but it was no good. He is beyond mortal aid. Nobody can help him. Nobody. But I must not tell him so.

The Light goes out on Evelyn and he leaves the platform

It is briefly dark and then the Light comes up slowly from dim to full to suggest the breaking day

At first, the platform is empty and then Evelyn enters carrying a large envelope

He pauses in front of the table and places the envelope upon it

When, as now, Reading Gaol is still uneasily asleep, I am aware of the difference in the passage of time in prison and in the world outside. Out in the world, time flashes by, sped by the excitement of event or the enjoyment of occasion. But, even here, the devouring tick-tock of time bears away the empty minutes down a stream of hours and days and months and years—each hour a season, each day a decade, each week an age, each month a millennium and each year an eternity.

The prison clock slowly strikes six. He goes and sits behind the table

Yes, even prison time, untouched by event, unwarmed by enjoyment, comes to an end. It is so with Oscar Wilde. (*He picks up the big envelope*) He leaves Reading Gaol today and is to take with him this envelope. It contains the venomous letter he has written to Lord Alfred Douglas and the Deed of Arrangement which cuts him off from his wife and children. I cannot see that either will benefit him. (*He discards the envelope*) The prisoners never cease to astonish me. You have seen Fingers Bennett. Would it surprise you to learn that he is a poet? He has written some verse about Wilde's release and he gave me a copy on condition I did not show it to Wilde. I think he is talented. You shall judge. (*He takes up a paper from the desk and reads*)
>What is your verdict now that you've seen
>The stupefying and the obscene
>Sameness of the prison routine?
>Shouldn't all of you thank your lucky stars
>That you're there (*he points*) and not here
>(*Jerking his thumb over his shoulder*) behind bars?
>Before you go hence, you should testify:

"There, but for the grace of God, go I."
Wilde leaves here today. What will he find?
That he'll be branded in a world unkind—
An outcast, a criminal, a liar,
Pederast, monster and pariah.
In a sad situation such as his,
You'd feel the world's against you (*he nods soberly*)
And it is.
(*He looks up*) Well, what do you think?

We are spared a reply for Oscar enters. He is dressed as we first saw him. There is one addition to his attire—he is wearing a silk hat

Evelyn turns over the poem and smiles in greeting. Oscar removes his hat and pauses, doubtless for effect

Evelyn (*rising*) You look very smart.
Oscar (*holding out his sleeve and regarding it critically*) Yes, not too bad. Still a fair fit, all things considered. What is to be done?
Evelyn If I could just tell you of the arrangements... (*He sits and his gesture invites Oscar to do likewise*)

Oscar sits, placing the hat carefully on the table

You will leave here with the Chief and Martin and they will escort you to Pentonville Prison where you will be officially released tomorrow. (*He produces a paper*) Would you please sign this as a receipt for money paid to you for work done while you have been here? (*He holds out a pen*)
Oscar Most certainly. (*He takes the pen*)
Evelyn And, while you are about it, kindly sign lower down the page for the Deed of Arrangement and the letter we so lately discussed.
Oscar (*completing the signing*) There you are. (*He throws down the pen*)
Evelyn (*taking a coin from a bag and passing it to Oscar*) And there you are.
Oscar (*ruefully contemplating the coin in the palm of his hand*) Thank you for small mercies. I can justly claim that I have never worked so hard for so little. (*He pockets the coin and rises*)
Evelyn (*rising also*) That is all. Those are all the formalities.
Oscar Then it remains for me to thank you for all your forbearance and for your many kindnesses. My sentence would have been much easier to serve if you had been in charge when I first arrived here. (*He offers his hand*) Thank you, Major Nelson.
Evelyn (*shaking hands*) Good luck, Mr Wilde. I shall be looking out for your next play.

Oscar I hope I won't disappoint you.

Evelyn now picks up the large envelope which he passes to Oscar

Evelyn In here is the Deed of Arrangement and also your letter to Lord Alfred Douglas. Once more, I ask you to think again about sending it to him—it can only cause trouble, distress, enmity.

Oscar (*weighing the envelope in his hand*) If anybody could persuade me, it is you. But I must hold to my purpose or I shall always regret it. (*He places the envelope beside his hat and then pauses, struck by a thought*) I shall see him soon. I shall see Bosie. (*His expression is troubled*)

Evelyn regards him with concern

Evelyn Are you all right?

Oscar Oh, yes. I was just thinking that there is no justice. In Heaven perhaps. Not here.

Evelyn You mean because you failed to get remission?

Oscar (*waving a dismissive hand*) Oh, that? No, no. There is something else. I have just realized that I, a self-confessed lord of language, have been ruined for life by a foul-mouthed marquis whose conversation is a social disaster, who has only a nodding acquaintance with grammar and can't spell! (*Clearly, he is ready to depart but, unaccountably, he still lingers*)

As if to bridge an apparent awkwardness, Evelyn speaks

Evelyn Well, there it is, Mr Wilde! It is finished! Your punishment is over!

Oscar Oh no, Major Nelson. (*He smiles*) By no means. Now it begins.

Oscar sweeps up his hat, claps it on his head and goes

Evelyn stands unmoving, looking after him and the revelation ends as the Light fades

FURNITURE AND PROPERTY LIST

Further dressing may be added at the director's discretion

ACT I

On stage: 2 small tables. *On table* C: water bottle, glass, slim volume, paper knife, pen, inkstand. *On table* R: lorgnette, fan, notebook, pencil, writing paper, pen, inkstand
3 chairs

Off stage: Walking stick (**Evelyn**)
Briefcase containing wad of correspondence (**Penelope**)
Large-size papers fastened by pink ribbon (**Evelyn**)
Notebook, pencil (**Penelope**)
Brief (**Evelyn**)
Bag (**Newsboy**)

Personal: **Oscar:** flower in buttonhole
Evelyn: revolver
Oscar: visiting card
Evelyn: spectacles
Newsboy: bill with headline "Lord Queensberry Not Guilty! Oscar Wilde Loses Libel Case!"
Newsboy: bill with headline "Queensberry Case Sensation! Oscar Wilde Arrested!"
Evelyn: barrister's wig
Evelyn: full-bottomed wig of a judge

ACT II

Set: On table C: papers, inkstand, pen, bundle of tracts, clipboard
On table R: paper bag containing pork pie. *Under it*: chamber pot

Off stage: Hoe (**Oscar**)
Plant (**Oscar**)

Briefcase containing document (**Penelope**)
Large envelope (**Evelyn**)
Paper (**Evelyn**)
Bag with coin (**Evelyn**)

Personal: **Evelyn:** packet of cigarettes, box of matches

LIGHTING PLOT

Property fittings required: nil
1 interior. The same throughout

ACT I

To open: Overall general lighting

Cue 1 **Voice**: "It is." (Page 25)
Fade lights out, bring up spotlights on **Evelyn** *and* **Oscar**

Cue 2 **Evelyn**: "…hard labour for two years." (Page 25)
Fade out spot on **Evelyn**

Cue 3 **Oscar**: "May I say nothing?" (Page 25)
Fade out spot on **Oscar**

ACT II

To open: Overall general lighting

Cue 4 **Oscar**: "What an artist!" (Page 30)
Fade lights down a bit

Cue 5 **Oscar**: "…were exercising in the prison yard." (Page 30)
Fade lights out, bring up spotlight on **Oscar**

Cue 6 **Voice**: "On report for talking!" (Page 30)
Bring up lighting

Cue 7 **Evelyn**: "Take that man away to solitary!" (Page 32)
Fade lights slowly

Cue 8 **Evelyn**: "The Judgement of Solomon…" (Page 32)
Black-out briefly, then bring up lighting to full

Cue 9	**Oscar:** "…the tension is unbearable." *Fade out lights, bring up spotlights on* **Evelyn** *and* **Oscar**	(Page 34)
Cue 10	Great outbreak of noise *Fade out spotlight on* **Evelyn**	(Page 35)
Cue 11	**Oscar:** "…for all us outcasts." *Black-out for a moment, then bring up full lighting*	(Page 35)
Cue 12	**Oscar** communes with Nature *Black-out for a moment, then bring up full lighting*	(Page 42)
Cue 13	**Evelyn:** "But I must not tell him so." *Black-out for a moment, then slowly bring up dawn lighting*	(Page 50)
Cue 14	**Evelyn** stands unmoving *Fade lights out*	(Page 52)

EFFECTS PLOT

ACT I

Cue 1   **Penelope** rises   (Page 5)
Waltz music in background, continuing

Cue 2   **Penelope** sits   (Page 8)
Fade out waltz music

Cue 3   **Evelyn** moves nearer to **Oscar**   (Page 9)
Street noises in background: horses hooves etc., continuing

Cue 4   **Oscar**: "… live to hear you preach a sermon!"   (Page 10)
Sound of hoofbeats and wheels near at hand

Cue 5   **Evelyn**: "Cab! Cab!"   (Page 10)
Sound of cab halting

Cue 6   **Evelyn** runs off   (Page 10)
After a moment, sound of cab starting and moving off

Cue 7   **Oscar** kisses **Penelope**   (Page 11)
Increasing applause

Cue 8   **Oscar** gestures to stop applause   (Page 11)
Applause fades out

Cue 9   **Oscar**: "…aroused by such a fanfare?"   (Page 11)
Laughter

Cue 10   **Penelope**: "…fame, vengeance, victory!"   (Page 12)
Outburst of applause

Cue 11   **Penelope** and **Oscar** exit   (Page 15)
Loud, sustained applause with cries of "Author! Author!" and "Bravo!"

Cue 12   **Oscar** holds up a hand   (Page 15)
Cut applause

Cue 13	**Oscar**: "…of the play as I do myself." *Laughter and applause, fade out when ready*	(Page 15)
Cue 14	**Evelyn** turns the page *Noise off stage*	(Page 19)
Cue 15	**Evelyn** studies the brief *Loud doom-laden* **Voice** *calls out off stage* *as script page 23*	(Page 23)
Cue 16	**Oscar**: "…except myself." *Laughter*	(Page 23)
Cue 17	**Oscar**: "I never do." *Outbreak of laughter, quelled by* **Voice** *calling* *as script page 24*	(Page 24)
Cue 18	**Evelyn**: "…why you did not kiss him?" *Echo effect: "Was that the reason… Was that the reason* *why you did not kiss him?"*	(Page 24)
Cue 19	**Oscar**: "…one is put in the pillory for it." *Outburst of applause, quelled by* **Voice** *calling* *as script page 25*	(Page 25)
Cue 20	**Evelyn**: "…of the charges laid against him?" **Voice** *as script page 25*	(Page 25)
Cue 21	**Evelyn**: "And that is the verdict of you all?" **Voice** *as script page 25*	(Page 25)
Cue 22	Black-out *Echo effect: "Nothing… Nothing… Nothing…"*	(Page 25)

ACT II

Cue 23	**Oscar**: "…Clapham Junction Railway Station." *Background noises, continuing: train whistles, engines* *shunting, carriage doors slamming, trains arriving* *and departing*	(Page 26)
Cue 24	**Oscar**: "…she doesn't deserve to have any." *Final shriek of train whistle to end train noises*	(Page 27)

Effects Plot

Cue 25	**Oscar**: "…and the prisoner behind me said." **Voice** *as script page 30*	(Page 30)
Cue 26	**Oscar**: "We all suffer equally." **Voice** *as script page 30*	(Page 30)
Cue 27	**Oscar**: "…visits the prisoner in his cell." **Voice** *as script page 32*	(Page 32)
Cue 28	Spotlights on **Evelyn** and **Oscar** *Sudden loud clanking noise*	(Page 34)
Cue 29	**Oscar**: "…ticking away." *Clock ticking, fading in a moment*	(Page 34)
Cue 30	**Oscar**: "I won't listen!" *Great outbreak of noise*	(Page 35)
Cue 31	Spotlight goes out on **Evelyn** *Cut noise, clock slowly strikes eight*	(Page 35)
Cue 32	Lights come up **Voice** *as script page 36*	(Page 35)
Cue 33	**Oscar** fetches the chamber pot **Voice** *as script page 36*	(Page 36)
Cue 34	**Oscar** stands deep in thought **Voice** *as script page 38*	(Page 38)
Cue 35	**Oscar** collects the chamber pot **Voice** *as script page 39*	(Page 38)
Cue 36	**Evelyn** enters *Outbreak of bird-song*	(Page 39)
Cue 37	**Oscar** settles himself in chair *Bird-song swells*	(Page 42)
Cue 38	**Oscar** composes himself to slumber *Bird-song ceases*	(Page 42)
Cue 39	**Evelyn**: "…each year an eternity." *Clock slowly strikes six*	(Page 50)

www.ingramcontent.com/pod-product-compliance
Ingram Content Group UK Ltd.
Pitfield, Milton Keynes, MK11 3LW, UK
UKHW021847210426
5322IPUK00022B/516